LURE FISHING

SALMO × POLAND

Lure Fishing
PRESENTATION & STRATEGY
by
Dave Pugh

Coch-y-Bonddu Books
Machynlleth

LURE FISHING
Presentation and Strategy

by Dave Pugh

© First published by Coch-y-Bonddu Books, 2014
   Reprinted by Coch-y-Bonddu Books, 2021

© Cover Illustration: Maurice J Pledger,
   courtesy of Bernard Thornton Artists, London

ISBN 978 1 904784 64 7

Published and distributed by
Coch-y-Bonddu Books Ltd, Machynlleth, Powys SY20 8DG
01654 702837
www.anglebooks.com

Printed in the UK by Biddles Books Ltd

CONTENTS

SECTION ONE – PRESENTATION

What is a lure? Why do fish take a lure? Why do fish ignore a lure? Location. Speed of retrieve. Size of lure. Colour of lure. Lure action.

Avoiding lures tangling the line. Smoothness. Changing cast direction. Matching the rod to the lure. Watch the lure. Practise, practise, practise. Distance casting.

Repeatability. Speed. The 'wobble'. Keeping a lure at the depth you want. Knowing the depth. How far away is that underwater structure? Changing retrieve patterns. Another note on speed. 'The killer pause'.

Understanding structure. Drop-offs. Main channel bottom. Near bank. Fishing the structure – far bank shelf and drop-off. Lure Control. 'On the drop' technique. Water clarity. Fishing the structure – the central channel. Dealing with snags. Fishing the structure – near shelf and drop-off. Weed. Bank access. Open water.

FOREWORD

Every so often a book comes along which isn't a collection of stories about 'What I caught'. Not that there's anything wrong with an author indulging himself (or herself) in what they've caught, because you can learn from such stories as well as straight instruction.

Dave Pugh's book looks in detail at the technical side of lure fishing. Any fool can cast a lure out and wind it in – I've done that (with mixed results) over the years. It is getting that lure to catch fish as often as possible that is important to all of us. Dave gives you the benefit of his long-term experience by examining every important aspect of lure fishing in detail. Remember this – a lure is not a real fish and because of this, the angler may at times be operating at a disadvantage compared to someone fishing with a natural bait. Dave can show you how to overcome any such disadvantage and show you the best way to get results when lure fishing is the only way to go.

Read Dave's book carefully and I'm sure you will increase your effectiveness. The lure will not have changed, but what you do with the lure most certainly will have.

Neville Fickling
March 2014

ACKNOWLEDGEMENTS

My lure fishing has been greatly enhanced by contact with many people, but some deserve special mention for their contribution to my understanding and experience of the lure fishing world. Others too merit my gratitude for turning this from an idea in my head into the book you are reading.

Dave Lumb was probably my very first lure fishing contact – he never failed to give solid advice, and as I made my faltering early steps along the lure road he often helped me to stay on track, later offering me sound views after seeing a rough draught of this book.

Since there is not enough room to mention all the different blokes over the years who have really helped me to push on, these are the ones I've fished with the most and who have made the greatest contributions to my progress. All are good friends and very fine anglers and each deserve a special thank-you: Seb Shelton, Michel Huigevoort, Tim Kelly, James Ashworth, Neil Roberts, and Dave Hilton – may we share many more great fishing days.

I'm indebted to Neville Fickling for his foreword: his words are a nice commendation from a pike angler of his high standing.

I am of course very grateful to Paul Morgan of Coch-y-Bonddu Books for publishing my book, and to Pete MacKenzie and Paul Curtis whose specialist skills in design and editing have turned a load of words on my computer's hard-drive into a great-looking book. Thanks also to Maurice 'Mole' Pledger for the use of his fine illustration on the cover.

And, without doubt, the greatest thanks are owed to the one person without whose patience and forbearance this book would never have been written – my wife Julia – who has to put up with my failure to deal with many household chores whilst I disappear from before dawn until long after dusk, many times throughout the year.

INTRODUCTION

There wasn't very much written about fishing with lures way back in 1989 when I caught my first pike on a lure. The occasional article in general angling magazines waxed enthusiastic about the subject but hardly ever contained anything genuinely helpful that I can remember. In fact I'd be inclined now to think that a lot of the stuff I read then was just plain wrong. It's been a long journey since those distant days – writing this over twenty years later, we have the Internet, can buy lures from all over the world, read about fishing with lures for many species of fish from virtually any part of the world, and communicate with anglers who share our passion from many countries. There is certainly a lot of information available these days, but it is of somewhat variable quality and just sifting through the sales hype is a daunting task. The Internet itself has no 'quality filter' – anyone can make a website with a few pictures of fish, and who is to say whether they are great expert fish catchers or just very lucky to live in a place where there are lots of fish?

So how do you sort out exactly what is sound information and what is just stuff written to fill pages or sell lures? Trial and error is the only way. Spending your time on your waters finding out what works for you and what doesn't – and along the way spending good money on all sorts of lures to see if you can catch fish with them. I've been through this process over the last umpteen years and of course I'm still going through it, but I have made sufficient progress for it not to be hit-and-miss any more. I now consistently catch fish with lures in all sorts of conditions from my local rivers and other waters, and now I'm going to explain how I go about it. I hope that you will be able to use the advice given here to reduce the amount of 'error' in your own process of trial and error. If you have already started lure fishing then you might have already realised that it is not quite as easy as some writers and lure catalogues suggest. You have to apply yourself more than just trying a different lure from time to time. I am aware that this book is not a complete reference work but nor is it meant to be. Rather it reflects my own experiences, and what those experiences indicate as being the most important aspects of fishing with lures. It's not a book about lure fishing but rather about catching lots of fish with lures – which is a different story altogether.

I have no speculative theories about lures and fish. Plenty of other writers seem to think that such ramblings are important, but I don't, because catching fish with lures is really not very complicated – although it is only after you have caught a lot of fish that you can truly appreciate that.

I will mention quite a few lures – not exactly to recommend them, but so you can check out precisely what I am describing for yourself. If I was forced to give up all the lures I currently use, I'm sure I could easily find others that would do the same jobs. Although I'd probably have to 'doctor' some of them, as I already have done. I have no sponsorship from tackle manufacturers, and no commercial interest in promoting any particular brand – I write about what I use. I certainly won't give you a long list of indispensable 'killer' lures, because any lure is only as good as the angler using it. The same applies to other tackle – all anglers have their favourite rods and reels and aside from mentioning a few basic points about how different choices can affect what you can do I won't be trying to persuade anyone to buy any particular rod or reel.

As you read the book, you'll notice that I don't mention that many specific lure techniques. If I had decided to cover everything in detail, I'd still be writing now and it would never be finished: new lures, rigging and tackle are constantly being developed. Also, although my experience has all been in fresh water, the basic principles outlined here apply to every lure fishing situation, with whatever lure and technique is being used, whether in fresh- or salt-water.

This book is essentially a practical guide to understanding lures, how to fish them properly, and how to learn to think clearly about what you are trying to achieve. It is based upon countless thousands of rod hours, over nearly twenty-five years of fishing, on waters that are not full of fish. It is strictly about casting and retrieving the lures and although there are some references to the use of a boat I have not covered specific boat techniques such as trolling or vertical jigging, which require more detailed description of boat control than actual fishing.

The advice I give is quite simple, it is proven and time-tested and I know that I can go out tomorrow and prove it to myself or to anyone else. It is all my own original work but the development of my successful approach certainly owes a lot to the many other lure anglers who I have fished with – the good, the bad and the ... well, you know what I mean. You will find some advice is unique (at least I have never seen it written anywhere else) but it is all solid stuff that works to deliver great sport again and again.

In essence, this book is the one that I wish I could have read when I started lure fishing.

Remember:

➤ There is no magical secret technique or lure that will guarantee your success, Trial and error is the only way you can learn how to best use your lures for the water and the conditions on the day.

Section One
PRESENTATION

When you first take up lure fishing, you are confronted with a bewildering selection of lures and many strange terms used to describe them all. What are all those lures for? What do they all do? Which are the best? How many different ones do you need? And that is before you even get a lure into the water!

What is a lure?

Before you start, you can cut through some of the hype and excitement by asking a simple question: 'What is a fishing lure?' Over the years I have read all sorts of fanciful notions about lures and just how or why they fool fish, but I'll try to avoid conflicting opinions and to encompass all of the many interpretations by keeping the answer simple. The essential requirement of all angling is to induce a fish to take a hook into its mouth, so my definition is: 'A fishing lure is a man-made device used to deceive a fish into taking a hook into its mouth'. That covers all fishing lures. So all the features of lures – colours, patterns, weights, shapes, sizes, actions, rattles or whatever, have some function supposedly connected with achieving that objective. I'll come back to some of these details later but first we have to think a little more about that definition of a lure.

With just a small alteration, this definition could easily describe an edible bait on a hook. So an obvious question arises: 'What is the difference between an edible bait and a lure?' And, the equally obvious answer is 'edibility' because we know that fish cannot live by eating lures. (You could also argue that they cannot live by eating edible baits with hooks in them.)

On my first visit to Holland I was astonished by the range of lures available in a tackle shop. I'd never seen anything like it and now over ten years later I've still never seen such a range in any UK tackle shop. The huge choice doesn't automatically help a beginner because working out what you really need takes time and experience. All you can do for starters is select lures that are within the weight range that you can cast with your rod, are the right size for your target fish, and will run at a depth to suit your waters.

What I'm getting at is that there is no essential difference between an edible bait and a lure. They are just hook presentations and should be considered purely in the context of attracting a bite from a fish. But, for the lure angler, the difference in terms of presentation is very important because predatory fish often prefer a moving bait, and that is when a lure offers many advantages over an edible bait.

I know that many predator anglers who use live or dead fish baits will find this assertion difficult to accept. They 'know' that you cannot beat a live roach or a dead mackerel, or whatever. But a live roach or dead mackerel is useless unless it is presented on the correct tackle, with the correct rigging, in the correct place. In every fishing situation it is not the lure or the fish bait that catches the pike, zander or perch (or shark, or cod or tigerfish), but the angler.

You can fix up natural fish baits in ways that enable you to retrieve them in the manner of a lure, but they are not as durable as a lure made of wood, metal or plastic. Generally, one hit from one fish or even a brief contact with an underwater obstruction will render them unusable, or at least requiring some repair work to allow you to carry on retrieving them as before. Whereas you can catch countless fish with a lure made of a hard material. You also have an almost infinite choice of size, shape, action, weight, buoyancy and colour available straight from the tackle shop. I'm sure that with enough determination and ingenuity an angler could devise all sorts of rigs to offer the same diversity with natural baits but it would be a slow old job and while he was messing around trying to get everything to work just right, the lure angler would be fishing. Also edible baits have to be looked after, kept cool, oxygenated or whatever, while the lure just waits in the box until the next time it is required – whether that is half-an-hour or half-a-year later.

Why do fish take a lure?

If you think of each retrieve of a lure simply as a presentation (in exactly the same way that static, edible bait is just a presentation) you can clarify your thinking considerably and make sound judgements about the usefulness of different lure choices. What lures offer is a huge choice in moving presentations, where just clipping on a different lure can completely change the presentation immediately. If the situation demands a static bait, then a natural edible bait will do just fine, but if a moving bait is required then a lure is the smart choice. The principal advantage in using a moving bait is that it can be shown to a lot more fish. So if you can make

Often this sort of picture is used to demonstrate how greedy a small fish is but what it really tells us is how poorly the fish sees the lure sometimes and attacks without getting the whole picture.

that presentation the right one, you can catch rather more fish than with a static bait.

Many anglers have asked the question: 'Why does a fish take a lure?' and many writers over the years have wasted whole forests of wood pulp speculating about the answers. These usually come from one of two standpoints – the first being that many lures look nothing like the natural food that the target predator eats. The second is that there must be some almost mystical quality in any given lure that could be discovered and used to make an even better lure. I've lost count of the number of times I've waded through pages of what is essentially guff.

Our target species are predators and eat fish, so why are they fooled into taking lures that often appear to bear little or no resemblance to fish?

To answer this, you should imagine what it is really like in the underwater world of fish. We have all seen wonderful wildlife films showing vividly-coloured fish swimming around coral reefs (in the lights from the cameras) but such ideal underwater viewing conditions are extremely rare in nature, apart from in very shallow water. In most waters, light (which will vary anyway

Another example of a fish only reacting to a part of the lure. This small zander is hooked on the rear treble of the Dawg, perhaps concentrating on that wriggling tail?

due to cloud cover and the angle of the sun) is diffused to a considerable degree by surface disturbance and suspended matter in the water. Consequently, the vast majority of fish in the vast majority of waters do not see the beautiful pictures of our nature films, but live in a dusky world of vague half-shapes and shadows. It is a world where automatic decisions about whether to flee from a potential predator or closely investigate a possible food source must depend upon very rapid interpretations of scanty information – survival hinges entirely upon these reactions.

A predator does not see a roach, a bream or a minnow, but just a shape (or part of a shape) that might be small enough to be something to eat. It then attacks, or not, depending on various conditions like its state of hunger, the proximity of the prey, an assessment of how likely its attack is to succeed, and its fear of exposing itself to attack – to name just four that come to mind quickly. I've obviously expressed all these conditions in rational human terms but there is no rational processing of data going on in the predator's brain. In reality the decision that follows – to attack or not – is not a decision at all but a reaction, a reaction that is programmed by millions of years of evolution. So the predator sees something, or part of something, reacts, and either attacks or not. From our point of view, we notice the reactions that result in the fish revealing itself, these might be a reassuringly solid take, a nudge on the lure, a swirl in the water behind the lure or just a glimpse of a pursuing predator. All are reactions provoked by the lure, and we do not see those reactions (and I'm sure there are plenty) where the fish doesn't show itself at all.

Having understood the harsh reality of life in the underwater world, and how predators react to lures (or anything else in the water), it becomes obvious that it is impossible to isolate any one magical quality in a lure – simply because what we see and know about the lure is just not what the predator is seeing. Sure the predator is reacting to something, but it could be to a whole lot of different and unrelated things. For instance, just the particular angle at which the fish first sees the lure may provoke a particular stimulus (like attack or reject) which could be different if the fish first sees the lure from a different position. And that is nothing at all to do with the lure itself, but just where you happen to be casting from in relation to the fish.

So when you pick up a beautiful lure and examine it closely, you are not seeing what the fish sees at all. Yet some part of that lure when you fish it, its movement or its position, perhaps, can provoke the same reaction from the predator that the half-seen partial shape of a prey fish does. And if you are doing your job right that reaction will be a take and a fish in the landing-net! That is why lures that resemble nothing that

Wildlife and angling artist David Miller took these underwater photographs in clear water and strong sunlight: you can identify many of the fish easily enough but many are obscured by refracted light, and others are at various angles to the viewer. The precise flat pictures that we see in books are not really accurate depictions of what fish are like at all. In nature they are a mixture of shapes moving in various directions and changing shape as they turn or move through changing light. A predator has to take its chance while it can. If it waits for a perfect opportunity to see a fish side-on in good light it will go hungry, and of course they make mistakes, sometimes not getting a good enough grip so the prey fish escapes. Sometimes, no doubt, predators grab sticks or leaves that move in the flow, and luckily for us they occasionally see a potential meal in a strangely-coloured, peculiarly-shaped unnaturally-moving lure.

David Miller's beautiful paintings can be seen at www.davidmillerart.co.uk

you will ever have seen swimming can be interpreted as prey, depending on just how the predator sees them.

You should also consider how we picture fish. An illustration or photograph of a roach in a book looks nothing like it does in the water. What a roach looks like in the water will vary dependent on water clarity, light levels and background.

Finally, if a predator does get a close look in clear water at an unfamiliar object that is food-sized, why should it not bite it? Fish don't have hands, and evolution has programmed them to test potential food sources in their mouths, otherwise they would never eat anything. Unless they have been conditioned to be cautious by repeated capture, then predators, even when not very hungry, are often driven by simple curiosity to check out a new opportunity.

Why do fish ignore a lure?

If a fish takes your lure then that is just wonderful – but when they don't take your lure, you should be asking the question: 'Why not?' Or, more usefully, 'Why are no fish taking my lure, right now?' Now you're getting serious about your fishing. You should be asking the question every time you make a retrieve and don't get a fish, because the answer is absolutely relevant and will really help you to catch fish. This is the big secret, the key question that successful lure anglers ask themselves whenever they are not catching. It's the one question that drives our development as lure anglers, and it's a question to which the answers are generally pretty straightforward and transparent.

Moving away from lures for a moment, I'd like to recount a little history and some important skills I learnt in my early fishing days.

I started fishing (for the first time without my father's guidance) as a young teenager in the early 1970s. I used to cycle down to the local River Severn at Winnals to watch the matches at weekends and to cadge any maggots that were left over. I saw some very skilful anglers fishing with fine tackle and stick floats which they used to catch roach, chub, dace, etc. I also used to read David Hall's *Coarse Fishing* magazine which had very helpful articles by great match anglers like Kevin Ashurst about fishing with the stick float. Eventually, when I could buy decent tackle I got pretty good at using a stick-float myself, so much so that Stourport tackle shop owner and England international, John White, once watched me catching some dace and said I was pretty good – which was high praise indeed. John had given me lots of advice over the years on my regular trips to his shop. I was never interested in fishing in matches, just in the skills required to build a bag of fish from a swim. I know that match anglers are hardly the friends of predator anglers, but if you want to see the highest degree of angling skills they are the ones to watch – with no choice over their swims they still have to deliver. No poaching, privileged access, rule breaking or fibbing about weights for them – the one who wins the most is undoubtedly the best.

The reason for this digression is to explain a little about stick float fishing – running a float through a swim on the river. One key aspect of this was loose-feeding maggots, which is of no direct relevance to us lure anglers beyond underlining the point that having some fish present is a basic requirement for success. The other part of the story though, is of vital importance … control. Getting that maggot and hook to go through the swim in exactly the right way to get the maximum number of bites required considerable skill. Setting the depth, holding the float back just so, moving a No.8 split shot an inch or two, and lots more little adjustments could mean the difference between success and failure. The quarry, often well-educated fish, could be extremely choosy about just how they wanted that maggot. There never appeared to be any reason why the fish needed to have the bait presented in just the one way – and the precise way varied from day to day – but as soon as you got it right you started catching. Knowing where the maggot was, just how it was behaving, and how to affect it: these were the vital skills.

As lure anglers we will only on very rare occasions need such a precise level of skill. But keep in mind those roach, and how they would refuse a juicy maggot that they could clearly identify as the same food they were eating. Then consider what we are asking of our quarry – to eat something that very often bears no particular resemblance to normal prey, and you'll realise that the key to success is the ability to get the lure into the right place doing the right thing.

So let's say you have just caught a nice fish and your fishing mate shouts over:

'What did you get that on?' So you tell him.

'What colour?' is his next question, and he searches through his box to find the matching lure.

But just think about it for a second. Simply knowing the lure without knowing anything else will not help him much. Your swim might be deeper, shallower, weedier or shadier than his. Your lure might be a really sensible choice to take account of the specific features of your swim, but a lousy one for his. More useful information would be:

'It took a slowly-rising crankbait that I had paused 5 ft down just before it ran into the 4 ft to 10 ft drop-off'.

The key information there is not the crankbait or the pause but the drop-off and the depth at which the fish hit. If one pike is using that feature then there will probably be others using that or similar features, and probably at a similar depth. There may be other lures that will do a good job along that drop-off. The crankbait may not matter much, but the pause may be important. And the next time you visit the water that drop-off will still be there and may again hold a fish or two.

Now just imagine how your fishing would change if when you arrived at the water you were given a 3D map with the position of every pike marked on it. You would stop worrying about the trivial details of your lures – you would be selecting purely on

Michel Huigevoort hurrying to the next spot. When fishing large waters you need a big boat for safety and comfort with an outboard big enough to get to the best areas quickly to maximise fishing time. Whilst on holiday In Sweden Michel travelled over 50 km a day in his boat to find good fishing.

the basis of getting the lure near to each pike. You would also not be spending time trying to catch every stray pike you could, but would be focusing all your efforts into presenting lures where there were concentrations of pike.

You are never going to get that 3D map – instead you have to build up your experience so you can make some predictions about the probable location of concentrations of predators – that is a key part of lure fishing. You have to go to the fish rather than waiting for the fish to come to you like a bait angler. And you can only learn about the underwater features and how predators relate to them by knowing exactly where your lure is in relation to those features. You can't do this in a few trips – it takes a long time and many trips at different times of year under different weather and water conditions to start to make sense of it all. But that is what you should be working towards – remembering which of your lures you caught a fish on is far less important than where it was when you caught it.

Location

Let's return to the question, 'why are no fish taking my lure right now?' The most likely answer is simply that there are no fish close enough to your lure. So lure choice is not a whimsical matter. It is not about your favourite, or 'what the fish want', but primarily about where the fish are. That is the first consideration in choosing your lure – get it wrong and you catch no fish.

Location is not just the right water or the right swim on that water or the right depth in that swim – it is a very precise place within the range that a fish can detect the lure and is willing to move to take it. You could have bells, whistles and flashing lights on your lure so that every predator for miles would be aware of it, but awareness doesn't mean they will all be racing towards you in their rush to take it. Getting the lure close enough to the fish is what location means. Your lure choice, then, has to match two essential requirements – can you cast it far enough? And, will it run at the correct depth?

Speed of retrieve

If all you ever do is to ensure that your lure is close to some predators you will get takes, often enough to make you feel like a pretty successful lure angler. Remember that you have absolutely no choice in this matter – if your lure is not close enough to a fish then you catch nothing. The most successful anglers go to considerable trouble and expense to make sure that they are close to their target fish.

There are, of course, other important factors affecting your choice of lure. Having found some fish, and got your lure amongst them, there is a second factor that will have a crucial bearing on your catches – the speed at which your lure is moving. You can retrieve your lure as slowly or as quickly as you want – no retrieve speed is too fast or too slow to get a take. Granted, a lure could be going simply too fast for a fish to catch up with, but this speed would be rather quicker than you could reel it in! From stationary, to as fast as you can go, is the lure speed range that you should be considering – which is quite a wide range. Most lures though are comfortable to use moderately slowly, so for most of the time most lure anglers are retrieving most of their lures at a very similar pace – which is comfortable for them to crank their reel handles while watching the lure's action. And sure, they do catch the fish that respond to the lures going along at that pace. But …

Most lure anglers miss out on a lot of fish because this steady, moderately-slow pace is the wrong one for a lot of fish a lot of the time. You really should try as wide a range of speeds as you can manage.

Remember that stationary lures also get taken. Almost every lure angler has some tales of fish hitting static lures, either while they are undoing a tangle or pouring a coffee or something, and they are all delighted and amused by these 'flukes'. Flukes? My eye! There are no flukes in fishing – everything is repeatable. A lot of things have to be right for a fish to take a lure, its position and its speed being the two most important. Sometimes zero is the right speed, and that is one of the reasons why anglers using static dead baits catch fish. At the other end of the speed equation is another 'fluke' – the fish that takes a lure when you are ripping it back in to clear a strand of weed from it. If you have decided that a slow-medium speed is always right, and that those fish that hit very fast or static lures are just amusing diversions, then you have to change your thinking.

It is vitally important to success in lure fishing that you base your judgement about what works purely upon your experience and not try to edit your experience based upon your opinion, or on someone else's opinion that you've read. Lure speed is the key variable and, after location, it is the most important thing that you can control to improve your fishing results. Annoyingly, it is often quite random – I cannot come up with any reason why speed matters so much. Why one day a fast retrieve is essential, then on another, in apparently identical conditions,

Small lures can keep you busy but I don't think it is very smart to teach small zander about lures. I'd rather they learned these lessons when they were much bigger.

the retrieve must be dead slow to get any interest. I just know they all have to be tried.

All the above can be condensed into the simple expression 'depth and speed' that you may have read about from time to time. I've expanded on it for a couple of reasons:

Firstly the phrase is often misinterpreted to mean that you should fish your lures deep and slowly – this is certainly not the case.

And secondly the right depth and speed depends on the fish and where they are. How they are positioned is affected by many things, including underwater structure, shoals of prey fish, light or shade and water clarity.

There is no one correct depth and speed: it varies from day to day and through the day as light and wind change, and from swim to swim and water to water. It is seldom obvious why the speed or precise depth should matter that much, but it really does matter, and when you get it right you will know about it because you'll be busy unhooking fish.

*Small pike take
very large lures
often enough,
unfortunately.*

Size of lure

After considering position and speed, the third most important
factor is the size of your lure. Lure size is a regularly-discussed
topic, but it's quite simple – under most conditions, on most
waters, bigger lures catch a higher proportion of big fish. Small
lures certainly catch big fish, but not as frequently as big lures
do. If you are targeting big fish then use the right size of lure.
Even with these big lures you will still catch a majority of small
fish so you won't get too bored waiting for a big one. From
my own direct experience of fishing for pike I know that with
small lures (up to about 4 in) maybe one pike in thirty will be
a 'double'. But with proper pike-sized lures (from 5 in up to
as big as you can buy), the ratio improves to as good as one
pike in three being a double (although most days you won't
catch as many pike in total). I know which I prefer! But if you're

Using small lures means having to unhook these little horrors far too often.

Using really outsized lures like this 13 in Grandma does make it hard for very small pike to hook themselves but does not provide any magic answer to catching monsters.

Three men in a boat: Two of them, Dave Hilton and me both using 4.5 in shads had both passed over this spot but the third, Dean Mallows had chosen the 6 in option. This golden 10 lb 6 oz zander nicely endorsed his opinion.

fishing a water where large pike are very scarce then the smart choice may be to use smaller lures. You'll just have to accept that you are reducing your already slim chances of a big pike but will at least have perhaps a better chance of other species like perch, zander, and chub. However, bigger lures also catch bigger perch, zander and chub. And although the smaller fish will still hit your big lures, their smaller mouths (compared to even very small pike) mean that fewer get hooked. You can use this to your advantage because when perch fishing, for example, a bigger lure will stay untaken in a shoal of small perch long enough for a bigger one to find it – and you cannot hook a big one whilst you are unhooking a little one.

That covers position, speed and lure size. These are the 'big three' variables that you can control to make sure you catch some nice fish fairly regularly.

Two other variables are colour and lure action, but they are quite peripheral – just a bit of fluff around the edges of what really matters, but strangely enough they are also probably the most talked-about lure fishing topics.

Colour of lure

Does colour matter? Yes and no! If you tell me that you have a colour of lure that you can't catch with (blue is often the one that suffers from this misconception), then I believe I could take it and catch a fish with it. If (and remember this is a big if) I can get it to where some fish are and can run it at a suitable speed. That doesn't mean that colour is irrelevant, it just means that it needs to be considered in context – the wrong colour choice will only on extremely rare occasions be enough to stop you catching any fish. I was amused recently looking at a website where a lure was available in 87 different patterns. Can you imagine the manufacturer's horror waking up one morning and suddenly realising that the existing 86 were not enough? Remember that fish never buy lures – only anglers do. So lures are painted to appeal to anglers. If you decide that a lure of a certain colour pattern is no good then it will remain unused in your box or hung up in your garage. Your opinion of its effectiveness will be proved right though – because it certainly won't catch any fish in either place.

Lure action

The first thing you notice with a lure once you get it into the water is its action. They wobble, wiggle, spin, glide or whatever, in various ways. It is very tempting to make a hasty judgement about how you feel about that action and how attractive you think it might be to a fish. This is a huge mistake. We all have personal preferences, but they are far more likely to restrict our choices than to expand them. What you feel about a lure's action is irrelevant, unless your dislike of that action prevents you from using it. Lures with actions that are less appealing to anglers tend not to get used, so predators do not see them very often and this might be very important when trying to catch fish that have been fished for heavily. The one really useful aspect of a lure's action is that it often does have a large bearing on the range of possible retrieve speeds, so a variety of actions gives you an easily-controllable variety of speeds and that is when an understanding of lure action can be very important.

I've often heard a lure action described as 'lifelike' but the only lures I've seen that look like fish in the water are those with no action. Fish, whether healthy, ill or injured, just don't wiggle very much in the water most of the time.

I've never noticed any correlation between water conditions and the effectiveness or otherwise of different lure actions in catching fish, and most of the time fairly gentle actions catch plenty. If different actions really mattered in attracting fish then surely it would be pretty straightforward to make such a correlation.

Remember:

- There is no essential difference between an edible bait and a lure.

- The principal advantage in using a moving bait is that it can be shown to a lot more fish.

- When you are not catching any fish on your lure ask yourself, 'why are no fish taking my lure, right now?'

- The most likely reason for failure is simply that there are no fish close enough to your lure.

- Most lure anglers miss out on a lot of fish because a steady, moderately-slow retrieve is the wrong one for a lot of fish a lot of the time.

- Under most conditions, on most waters, bigger lures catch a higher proportion of big fish.

- The wrong colour choice will only on extremely rare occasions be enough to stop you catching any fish.

- What you feel about a lure's action is irrelevant to the fish.

We start the control of our lure with the cast. Anyone with a few hours' fishing experience will be able to get their lure somewhere out into the water – after a fashion – but only practice will improve your distance and accuracy. There are a few points I will cover here that may be helpful, and probably the smartest advice is to practice smoothness and tidiness before trying to achieve maximum distance.

Some lures cast much further than others. It is not only their weight that affects that distance, a compact lure like a small jerkbait will fly a long way in a nice straight line, but a crankbait with a big lip, or a light-gauge spoon, will not. This can lead to problems and when I hear of lure anglers getting continual tangles with such and such a lure and complaining about its design, be assured that it is not the lure, it is the angler's casting technique that is at fault. Different lures need adjustments in casting methods (sometimes quite subtle ones) to prevent tangling problems.

Avoiding lures tangling the line

A lure tangles with the line (or more usually the leader) in two ways. Firstly, as it decelerates on the second half of the cast, the lure slows down and turns with its hooks fouling the wire. It is straightforward to fix this problem – you just have to 'feather' the line as soon as the lure starts to slow. With a multiplier, just lightly touching the line drum with your thumb does it. With a fixed-spool reel (something that anyone who has ever float-fished with light line would have learned very quickly) you let your index finger drop lightly towards the lip of the spool, where you can feel the coils of line brushing your finger-tip –

with practice and experience again, you do this automatically. Not only will this straighten the line out in flight and prevent the lure from tangling but it will also stop loose line tangling around the reel.

The second (and most frequent) cause of tangling happens when your floating lure lands with its front end pointing away from you, the wire leader sinks, and as you tighten up you pull the leader back under the lure and through the trebles. I've fished with a few anglers who have had this problem and it took me a while to work out why they were tangling, and I was not, when we were using the same lure and similar tackle. It is fairly simple to fix even though it is quite subtle – just have the rod pointing at the lure as it splashes but instantly pull the rod tip gently sideways a foot or so while the line is still slightly slack to neatly turn the lure around without pulling the leader under the lure. This also conveniently straightens all the line between the guides before you engage the pick-up or close the bail arm. A sudden strong pull immediately after the lure splashes down (to get a floating lure to dive sharply) will frequently cause these tangles – a gentle start to the pull however will turn it around and prevent the problem.

Smoothness

The first requirement of consistent accurate casting is smoothness. All rods have an optimum casting weight range, and if you try to cast lures outside this weight range, or at the extreme ends of that range, you may create problems for yourself. You should load the rod with the weight of the lure on the back cast and let the bend in the rod accelerate it as the rod goes forward – don't strain for extra range. First thing to get right is the length of line between the rod tip and the lure. It does not have to be a fixed length for all lures. You can get a good caster to cast even further by slightly increasing this length (albeit at the cost of a little accuracy) but a poor caster will not respond well. You should experiment to get this length right, with experience it is something that comes automatically for every lure.

The first outings with a multiplier reel can be fraught for someone (like me) raised on a fixed-spool. It is important to read the instructions that come with your new reel. If you follow them carefully, they will keep you out of trouble while you feel your way. It is very important not to try to cast too far at first, until you can feel what is going on and instinctively adjust your thumb's braking pressure on the drum – this will take you a while.

You might find all sorts of tricks to speed up a multiplier for longer casts but it is important to learn to walk before you try running. And anyway, some esoteric reel tweak that adds a couple of feet for an expert tournament caster with a 6 oz lead at 180 yards, is not going to have any relevance to you casting a lure that wouldn't go further than 30 yards if you fired it from a cannon!

Swapping lures can often cause a problem because of the different casting characteristics of different lures. After an hour with a spinnerbait, the first big heave with a jerkbait is in some danger of getting into the far bank trees. Changing back from the jerkbait to the spinnerbait risks a big backlash when the reel drum continues spinning at the same rate while the lure slows down in flight. So take care and think about what you are doing. It is smart to make the first couple of casts with a changed lure gentle ones until you get a feel for its weight and casting behaviour.

Changing cast direction

Changing casting direction is another common cause of casting difficulties. If you have been letting fly with the wind behind you, it will all have become so easy as the line flies out, but turning into the wind and trying the same trick will immediately have you in big trouble. First casts, into the wind, need to be steady and carefully controlled until you adjust your technique to get the best from the lure.

Matching the rod to the lure

Casting works so much better if you are careful to match the rod to the weight of lure you are using. Firstly, read what the rod manufacturer claims, and then use your own judgement to find out how accurate that claim is. Be careful though, it will be immediately obvious if you are using too light a lure because it will not load the rod enough and you just won't get enough lure speed to pull much line from the reel. On the other hand, too heavy a lure might appear to be OK under normal use, but the one time you strive to add a few precious feet to reach a far bank swim, the extra load will suddenly prove too much for the rod and it will break. I did manage to do this once using a lure that was heavier than the rod's rating. It is an unpleasant experience and it took quite a while afterwards before I was brave enough again to load a rod up to its limit.

Watch the lure

No matter what type of reel you are using you should never look at your reel while you cast – or after the lure has splashed down. Whilst the lure is in flight, you should be checking that it's not going to hit the far bank, overhead cables and branches, ducks, swans, boats or whatever. Then when the lure is in the water, you should be watching it, or where it splashed down, or the line as it sinks. If a fish hits as soon as it splashes down (and it happens often enough to be worth several fish most seasons to me) you will be ready to strike. If a fish does not take the lure but maybe swirls under it, at least you will see it and be aware of its presence. And if that lure is a sinker, keep watching the line as you count it down. Sinkers get taken on the drop often enough, and even if you miss the take it might be a clue that fish are shallower than you thought – so on the next cast stop the countdown where you had the take and try a retrieve at that depth.

You sometimes get line bedding down into the spool, which

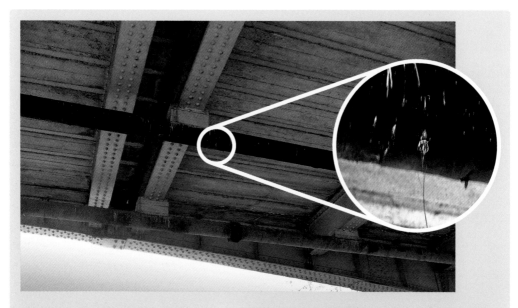

What's that hanging down under the bridge? How did that get up there? I'd have a job to do that if I was trying. If you watch where the lure is going and stop it if it's heading for trouble you can avoid these expensive mistakes.

A momentary lapse of concentration or a 'difficult wind'? Well the wind was James Ashworth's excuse for casting his Shallow Invader high into the willow. Good job we were on the boat, and the lure was easily retrieved – after I'd stopped laughing.

The Shallow Invader retrieved from its lofty resting place.

can abruptly stop a cast. This will often happen if you have been pulling hard on a snag, so you just have to take it easy with the first couple of casts after pulling on any snags.

Check what is behind you before you cast. Bushes and trees on the bank will mess everything up. Be aware of spare rods sticking up in a boat, and your boat partner should also be avoided. I have twice managed to hook a spare rod from the bank behind me and cast it into the River Avon, and I've had my hat hooked twice by one boat partner – incidents that are perhaps amusing in hindsight but not at all so at the time.

Practise, practise, practise

Casting is about practice, and if you put in the time you can get very, very good and impressively accurate at distance with hardly a tangle. Accuracy also takes time and effort. I often have less experienced boat partners comment on how 'lucky' I am with my casts because the lure just misses a branch or stops a few inches short of the bank, but after a while they usually realise that it isn't luck. I am aiming at small targets – dropping a couple of yards short of a branch is safe because

A 5 lb 6 oz Severn chub caught 21st October 2010. I was casting a jig for zander and I counted the lure down expecting it to hit the clay river bed in 11 seconds. I got to ten when I saw the line move in a way that it shouldn't have done so I struck. As soon as your lure is in the water you are fishing – you have to concentrate the whole time to make the most of your opportunities. A lure sinking through the water is just as valid a presentation as the lure being retrieved.

you'll never get caught on it. But on countless occasions it has been essential to get in very tight, so I aim for the exact spot where I want the lure to land. Now and then a cast goes awry but, fishing from the boat, so what? I can close-in and get the lure back. Applying a little common sense here, it is smart to make a couple of shorter casts first, so if the first attempt to get tight goes horribly wrong you are not moving the boat into shallow water over fish that you haven't covered.

Technically, it is best to start accurate casting by a simple forward cast, lining your wrist up directly onto the target, the rod tip following the line of your hand movement. If you take care to get that alignment right then all you have to worry about is range. When I'm working around bankside trees with

Dean Mallows demonstrating a perfect cast tight to the far bank of a canal just missing the overhanging bush. On a canal many of the casts are of very similar length and your confidence and accuracy builds as you 'get your eye in'. Sticking to the same lure helps a lot. When you change lures you should allow a bigger margin of error to begin with until you've got used to the different casting characteristics of the new lure.

overhanging branches, I do sometimes use more awkward sideways casting angles, because sometimes it's the only way to get a lure tight into a difficult spot. These casts are far more likely to go wrong than the straight casts but look spectacularly good when I pull them off. It's all practice – even when fishing open water you can still practice accuracy by aiming at floating leaves or bubbles – it doesn't cost you a lure if you miss them and it all adds to your competence.

Distance casting

A final word of caution, on some waters, especially big stillwaters, range really matters. Try not to give 100% every cast. Choose the best casting lures you can (which won't necessarily be the heaviest) and remember that getting a lure into the right place is far more important than exactly what the lure is, then keep it all smooth and take regular breaks. A repetitive strain injury to your shoulder or elbow can be very painful and can take a long time to recover from, and may mean sick leave as well if your job involves any manual work. After you have made the cast, your retrieve has to control the speed and the depth of your lure. Depth and speed are the two key factors in determining how many fish will take your lure, so you have to learn to be in control of both. You cannot control where the fish will be, but if you can control where your lure goes, you can choose lures and techniques that enable you to check out the places where they may be.

Remember:

- Practise smoothness and tidiness in your casting before trying to achieve maximum distance.
- How to avoid lures tangling the line.
- How to change directions.
- You must match the rod to the lure.
- Watch the lure not the reel.
- Practise is the key.

Repeatability

The essence of what we are trying to achieve when retrieving a lure is repeatability. If you get a fish, the most vital information is not what lure you were using but where the take occurred – so you need to know where your lure was when the fish hit it. Its depth and distance from your casting position are the two obvious things you should know, of course, but it might also be useful to know that it is adjacent to a weed bed, or a sudden change in depth (a drop-off), a sunken tree, or something else relevant to why that fish might be there. As lure control is mastered the lure also becomes a feature finder – not only are you catching fish but you are also reading the underwater structure from the information that is coming back up your line. If you do not know where your lure is, then you cannot make any sense of this information, and getting a take is an isolated event that does not shed any light on how you might get another – it is just luck. This lack of knowledge and reliance on luck can make you feel dependent on a certain lure or a certain colour, whilst the key information is ignored.

Every time you make a cast you are asking the simple question: 'Will a fish take this presentation?' But each cast can answer many more questions than that. Answers which will give you important information about the swim, then when a fish gives you a nice 'yes' you can fit that information into your knowledge of the swim. Knowing where the lure is means you can build this information into a rough 3-dimensional picture of the hidden world under the water's surface.

Knowing your lures is the first part of the information

With its compact shape and no lip, this Salmo Floating Slider is not so heavy that you need a heavy rod but it will cast accurately a long, long way. That can be very useful when you are standing on the bank of a huge gravel pit. If there is shallow water and patchy weed at long range this can be a useful presentation. It is easy to repeat the presentation too because the lure works in a very narrow depth band so you only really have speed to worry about. Although it turns easily from side-to-side that is not the only way to retrieve it – sometimes a less energetic, straighter retrieve catches more fish.

gathering process because each lure has its own sinking or diving rate, so at a given speed, at a given distance, with a given line diameter and a given rod tip position, a lure will run at a given depth. None of those 'givens' though, are given at all, you must control them.

Speed

Let's look at speed first. Using a crankbait that floats at rest but dives when retrieved, you will notice that it dives deeper if you crank it faster. At least it does so up to a point – each crankbait has a maximum depth that it will reach, and a maximum speed at which it can be retrieved. This is dependant to some extent on your tackle, but primarily dictated by its design – that is its size, shape, length and angle of its lip and the material it is made from.

To achieve its maximum depth a crankbait must run 'true', that is, not veer off to one side as it is retrieved. This tendency to veer off to one side is more pronounced as the retrieve speed is increased, and can be so bad that the lure corkscrews thought the water or kites up to the surface. This can usually be corrected with a little adjustment. Often this is just a matter of slightly – very slightly in fact – bending the eye that you clip your leader to in the opposite direction to the way the lure is running off. Some crankbaits have instructions for doing this on their packaging – just remember that a tiny adjustment is all that is usually required. As a crankbait ages and bears the scars of countless battles, it is more likely to start misbehaving in this way. Sometimes the whole body may have become distorted by too many encounters with fish and landing nets and no amount of bending the eye will fix it – it is time to retire it and replace it.

The 'wobble'

You can easily feel from the frequency of the wobble coming through the rod that you are keeping to a certain retrieve speed – higher frequency equals faster speed. So once your crankbait is at the depth you have chosen then it is not unreasonable to assume that it should stay at that depth as you retrieve it. Sadly, this is not the case.

The line angle between the lure and the surface of the water will also have a bearing on the depth, because the lure's lip will tend to settle pointing about 90° downwards from the line. At long range with quite a flat angle, the pull from the retrieve comes from almost directly in front of the lure, so it has the maximum effect and pulls it down well. But as the lure dives and gets closer to the rod, the line angle changes – the pull from the line is partly upwards, which pulls the nose of the lure up and so counteracts the diving effect from the lip,

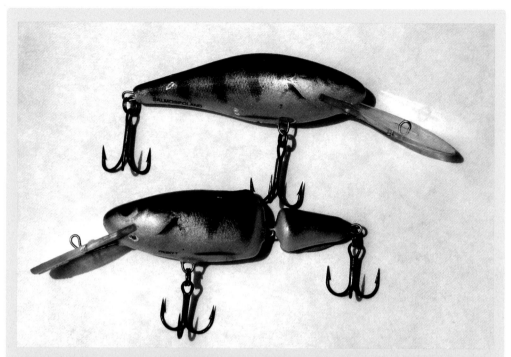

Jointed crankbaits are useful when you want a slow presentation. You can be confident that even at slow speed the Salmo Frisky 7 is going to be wobbling strongly. You can easily feel it through the rod, so it is easy to read and control the retrieve speed. The straight Salmo Executor 7 (top) is much easier to feel on a faster retrieve. I've caught many fish of all species on these lures but their small size (the '7' means 7 cm overall, including lip) makes them most useful for chub and perch.

so the crankbait runs shallower. To maintain the crankbait's depth, you have to keep the line angle the same throughout the retrieve. It is impossible to do this precisely, but you can mitigate it to some extent by lowering the rod tip as the lure gets closer. It looks very cool and polished keeping the rod tip low all the time but you should have it in the right place – low for running the lure deep, and high for keeping it shallow. It is just a small point that can make a huge difference to the control and effectiveness of your lure presentation. It is simple to do and it works, and it applies to all lures.

This mid-double pike would have swallowed the 8 in Swim'n Joe if the hooks hadn't stopped it. I had tweaked this lure by attaching smaller split rings and lighter gauge hooks to reduce the sink rate. With my rod tip high I can retrieve it very slowly around 2 ft below the surface so it doesn't wobble – this slow 'dead-stick' retrieve can be very effective in clear water such as in gravel pits or winter rivers if the pike won't respond to normal presentations. It is much easier to persuade yourself that a no-action lure will catch fish if you use one that resembles a fish, but this lure would not fit into the 'good lure' category because it is too fragile, so I only use it on special occasions when I know it isn't going to get shredded by jacks.

Keeping a lure at the depth you want

It is a good exercise when fishing reasonably deep water to practice retrieving a spoon or spinnerbait so that it keeps its depth right back to your casting position, or as close as you can before lifting it over the near bank ledge, or weed. If it comes to the surface too far in front of you, adjust your rod angle to get the tip down which will keep the lure down. (With a sinking lure you will also have to slow the retrieve a little as well.) This is most often of relevance when fishing from a boat. Fishing from the bank with a shallow margin it may be no bad thing to have the lure rising as it comes through shallowing water. Just be aware of the difference between the two situations, make the decision, and do it right.

Line diameter at least doesn't change as you retrieve your lure. Quite simply a thinner line (and leader) allows the lure to run deeper, because there is less drag from water pushing on thin line. Note that with smaller lures the attachment clip must be smaller as well – if it is too big it will impair the lure's performance. With pike-sized lures this is not much of a factor when fishing from the bank but it is of great importance when trolling, as using thinner line allows the lure to run deeper. You do notice the effect more when casting smaller lures. It can be very marked, so you may think you are using the same presentation as another angler using the same lure, but the running depth can be significantly different. Line smoothness also has a bearing on this – some modern braided lines are much smoother than normal braids and this makes a small but noticeable difference because they are less affected by drag from the water, allowing the lure to run a little deeper.

With sinking lures, those 'givens' are, of course, just the same as with lures that float, except that speed has the opposite effect – the faster the retrieve then the shallower the lure will run.

Knowing the depth

In order to choose a sensible depth to try with your lure, it is useful to know how deep the water is. For a boat angler, the sonar at least gives the depth directly beneath the boat (or more strictly speaking directly beneath the transducer), and for a bait fisherman there is always straightforward plumbing with a big weight and a float. The lure angler however has another way of checking depth – by casting out a sinking lure and seeing how long it takes to hit the bottom. As the lure sinks it pulls the line slightly tight, but as soon as it comes to rest, the line falls slack, so it is easy to just count the time it takes to sink to the bottom. When it is very windy the tension on the line from the wind can disguise this, so you need more weight – or it is perhaps best to wait for a calmer day.

This method is fine for checking relative depths around a swim, i.e., we know that over there it takes 8 seconds to hit the bottom, and over here it is just 5 seconds. But if you require more precise information – say a measurement in feet (which can be useful if you already know the working depths of your other lures) – we need to know the sink rate of the lure. To find the sink rate of the lure we have to know how deep the water is. This difficulty is easily overcome – just find somewhere with deep water tight to the bank, lower the lure until it hits bottom and then wind the line in until the rod tip is at the surface of the water with the lure just resting on the bottom. Now lift the rod – the amount of line (plus leader) between rod tip and lure is the depth. Now drop the lure back in on a loose line and count how long it takes to sink to the bottom, divide the depth in feet by the seconds you count before it reaches the bottom and that is the sink rate – it's that simple. Now you can cast all around you and learn about the underwater contours of the swim, but bear in mind that any current will increase the time it takes for the lure to sink.

Knowing the depth is very important – it can of course help you locate fish, but it is vital in judging the depth that your lure runs at. Take a sinking lure for starters: cast out, count it down to the depth you want to run at (you will of course have checked its sink rate previously in an area of known depth) and retrieve at a rate that will keep it at that depth. But how do you judge the speed of the retrieve? This is where knowing the depth of the water is so vital. Say your water is 8 ft deep, you cast, allow the lure to sink for four seconds (say the lure sinks at one foot per second) and then start cranking. To check that the speed is correct for maintaining the depth, just stop cranking and count how long it takes for the lure to hit the bottom – if it takes 4 seconds then you must be running pretty close to your original 4 ft countdown. Any less and you are cranking too slowly, any more and you are cranking too fast.

This might sound like a lot of work, but it is so important to get these things right. It will become an instinctive part of your fishing – but only with lots of practice. It is also one of the reasons why many experienced lure anglers try to use just a few familiar lures for much of their fishing. Being able to control the depth and speed without having to work too hard on it, means you can concentrate on fishing, thinking about your options instead of constantly struggling to keep different lures under accurate control.

You can do the same thing in reverse with a floating-diving crankbait. Learn how quickly it rises when you stop cranking, then you only have to pause the retrieve for a few seconds to check the running depth by counting how long it takes to reach the surface.

How far away is that underwater structure?

The importance of depth control should be apparent by now, but it is only one component of the three-dimensional position of the lure. How far away is it? With floating lures, it is easy enough to stop cranking and allow the lure to rise to the surface to check its position, but this is crude and of limited value because you want to know its position in relation to submerged objects. Just imagine you've made your cast, controlled the speed and depth well, and at some point in the retrieve you've felt the lure make contact with something inanimate. You get the lure back and see that there is a small strand of weed hanging from the front treble. So now you know there is a weed bed out there somewhere. There may be fish close to or inside that weed bed, and picking weed up on the lure is not the best way to try to catch them. Where was that weed bed? You didn't get the lure stuck in the weed, so you can assume that you only skimmed the top of it, so you know how high up in the water the weed reaches – if you knew your lure's running depth on that retrieve. But how far out was that weed? Cast to the same spot and try exactly the same retrieve again, but this time count the turns of the reel handle. If after, say, 18 turns you feel the bump as you nudge the weed bank again, bring the lure back and clean it off again. Repeat the cast, this time after say 16 or 17 turns you lift the rod tip to bring the lure over the weed, and … well, maybe you'll get a fish, you certainly won't catch the weed. Depending on what lure you are using you have lots of options. You could pause a floating lure to let it rise up over the weed, or do the same with a suspended lure to hold it in place for a few seconds. You could give the lure a twitch, or whatever. But you now have a vital piece of information – one that you can use to help you catch a lot of fish, and save you from a lot of lure weed-cleaning. Keep that spot in your memory, because when you return to the swim a week later the weed bed won't have moved. It may have grown a bit, but it will still be there. The same applies to snags or sudden depth changes. With experience you don't really count, you just do it automatically, but this 'count back' is a smart way to learn about swims.

Changing retrieve patterns

There was a hint there that a pause in the retrieve is sometimes the moment when a fish hits the lure. Sometimes you might

Between the snow showers, on 1st March 2006, the Avon pike were very lively, demonstrating that fast retrieves work just as well in winter if the water is clear enough and once you have found active fish. This 21 lb 12 oz pike took a spinnerbait fished quickly over the remnants of a summer bed of lily pads after I'd already covered the area slowly and carefully with a Squirrely Burt for a couple of small pike.

Yet on the same day, in another swim, James Ashworth caught a 20 lb 12 oz pike on a 'dead-stick' retrieve, and later in the day I caught this fish again on a pull-pause retrieve with a Squirrely Burt. This fish was absolutely stuffed with small fish, you could feel them individually in its belly. In normal trim it might only have gone 16 lb. It was apparently the only pike near a mass of preyfish and what was remarkable was that it was still apparently hungry.

think about the pause as 'triggering' the hit. Changes in your retrieve pattern are important, and pauses are the most consistently productive changes. And you should learn what the lure does when manipulated with the rod, or when you retrieve it at different speeds, and see how you can use those changes in different circumstances. It is plain old experience again, so repeat what works – always remembering that nothing works if you are not near any fish.

Another note on speed

Lure speed is the other side of lure control. Always be aware of how fast you are retrieving. If you get a fish you need to be able to repeat the retrieve at the same depth and speed. You have to mentally 'lock on' to the retrieve speed and not let it change accidentally. Many lures are going to be very hard to retrieve quickly for very long. You will get worn out just trying, so you have to find another lure that is easier to retrieve at the same depth and speed to sustain your effort. It is easier to maintain faster retrieves with stiffer rods that do not bend around too much as the lure fights back – and a larger reel can reduce the strain on your cranking hand.

While fast retrieves can be very tiring, slow retrieves are undemanding physically but require mental discipline to maintain them. One of the biggest problems when trying to maintain a slow retrieve is that you tend to speed up just before the end of the retrieve as the imperative of the next cast distracts you. Before long the slow retrieve has morphed into a medium-slow retrieve and its effectiveness has gone – so stay focused. When retrieves are required at the extreme ends of the speed range, it can be difficult to maintain the effort, so take a regular break, a coffee, a sandwich, or whatever, just to keep your head clear.

'The killer pause'

Have you ever had a pike swirl at the lure just as you lifted it from the water? It really makes you jump, especially if the pike launches itself two feet out of the water to grab the spinnerbait hanging there while you decide where to cast next – it is often described as all part of the glorious spectacle of lure fishing. It's actually a sign of lousy lure fishing technique. A pike that is trying that hard to get your lure should not be too hard to catch but usually, after they have made their big effort and failed, they don't come back.

So there is one thing you should do on every retrieve. I call it 'the killer pause' and it's a technique that will ensure that when a pike makes that big late charge, you have the lure in a position ready to react and set the hooks to get in control of the pike quickly at close range. It is very simple to achieve – as your lure comes close to the rod tip, just before it comes into view, pause and let it drop back for a couple of seconds. An eager following pike will generally not refuse the opportunity – it's the killer pause. The clearer the water then the further away you should do it. It's best to get them to take the lure before they start to worry about the big silhouette on the bank or on the boat. I think that if you can see the lure you've maybe left it a bit late, but sometimes it is unavoidable. You could mark your line with an indelible pen at say, 20 ft from the leader, to warn you that you are getting close to the time to pause. This simple and straightforward late pause catches me between ten and twenty per cent of my pike when casting, and these slow followers are often good quality fish that are perhaps less keen to rush in the moment that they see the lure. I've told boat partners about this and they've ignored it, only to be severely startled when a big double tries to climb into the boat trying to get hold of the lure – so they do get the hang of it eventually. Of course, if you'd prefer to see big pike swirling, jumping and slashing at the lure without giving you the inconvenience of having to unhook them then please ignore this advice. This killer pause just before the end of the retrieve also applies to perch – especially bigger ones.

These are the essentials of lure control, and if you ignore any of them you will catch fewer fish – now we'll look at how those controls are applied on the water.

Remember:

- Knowing your lures is the first part of the information gathering process.
- You can judge your retrieve speed by the frequency of a lure's 'wobble'.
- You need to learn how to run your lure at the depth you want.
- Always use 'the killer pause' at the end of every retrieve.
- Count the turns of the reel handle to 'count back' and learn about your swim.

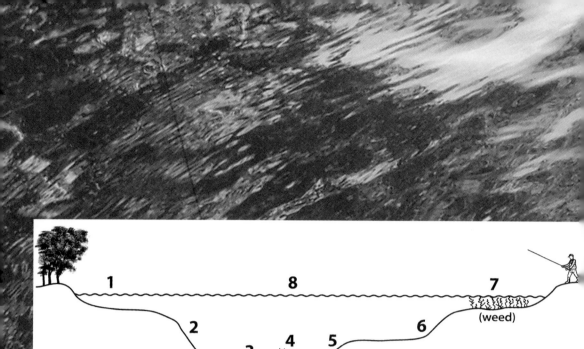

1 Far bank shelf in shade   5 Secondary drop-off
2 Far bank drop-off   6 Near bank drop-off
3 Bed of main channel   7 Near bank shelf
4 Submerged snag (branch)   8 Open water over main channel

Figure 1   *A typical cross-sectional view of a large river with a shelf against both banks.*

Understanding structure

Have a look at Figure 1. You'll find some variation like this along most large rivers and similar features will be present in some form on all types of water. The depth on each shelf will vary – between 2 ft and 6 ft is good – shallow enough to grow weed if not shaded, deep enough to hide a fish unless the water is very clear. The distance that the shelf sticks out into the river also varies – the further the better, because it allows more space for pike to congregate, so you might find good numbers there. And not just pike, all fish species use the shelves at different times. I've caught zander on them in less than 18 in of water when they were tucked under the remains of a small fallen branch. Chub will be cruising on shelves if they are not disturbed by anglers, and odd perch can be anywhere.

Drop-offs

Drop-offs (or sharp slopes) are fish motorways – they form the routes that fish use to move along the river and are very important. They are the fast routes into shallow water for pike and other predators, so when they want to move into the shallows they will turn up near the drop-off first. It is also where I've found it most likely to find shoals of perch, at all depths from the edge of the shelf down into the main channel. Zander will often sit tight into the bottom of the drop-off – sometimes at the edge of the top of the shelf and very occasionally a little way off it over the main channel. The depth at the end of the shelf, the steepness of the drop-off, and the depth at the bottom are crucial indicators as to what species you might find there and may vary seasonally and as water clarity changes.

Main channel bottom

The bottom of the main channel can hold fish of any species, although if chub are down there they don't often take lures. On the rivers I usually fish, pike will tend to be found singly near the riverbed rather than in groups. If they are 'ganged up' they will usually be high in the water, although gangs of pike moving along the river will almost always use the bottom of the drop-offs. Zander can be anywhere where there's a hard riverbed. Although the outside of even the slightest bend will usually hold more than the inside. They are very picky about flow and even on waters where the flow is barely noticeable, they will find the maximum flow for their daytime lies. Big sunken branches can be magnets for zander, although they also seem to ignore many that look suitable on the sonar. You don't have to fish into the snag – around it and, most importantly, over it is where you'll catch good zander, only the tiny ones are hiding inside it. Small groups of perch will also hang around these snags, although along the drop-off seems a more favoured location for bigger shoals.

Near bank

The near ledge here is not in the shade and has some weed on it. As a rough guide the more weed there is along the river the less important it is and you might never find an outstandingly good area. If you can get to look at weed beds with sonar you can shorten the odds of finding a productive area – the closer the weed is to the deep water of the central channel, the more pike will use it. The absolutely perfect weed bed runs right out to the edge of the shelf then stops abruptly because the drop-off is steep and the bottom of the drop-off is too deep for

Big sunken branches are both a hazard for stealing our lures and a blessing for providing homes for fish. This one that I pulled up with the lure retriever had not been in the river for long, so it had not found a permanent resting place. It would be gradually moved along the bed by the flow until it caught on either an existing snag or against a ledge and then it might become part of the river's permanent structure, or perhaps get swept away in the next flood.

weed. The least productive weed bed is on a gentle slope with no drop-off to bring the pike close.

Fishing the structure – far bank shelf and drop-off

Now let's fish all these features. The far bank ledge may be difficult to fish with a lot of subtle control needed simply because of its distance from you. You have to have a lure that can be cast far enough – some of your most useful shallow water lures like light spinnerbaits or shallow-diving crankbaits might not make the distance. The far bank ledge might be anything from 2 ft to 8 ft deep on my local waters so I don't really want to make a huge splash when my lure lands. In deep water it doesn't matter, a large splash may even draw fish, but I'd prefer not to scare the daylights out of any fish lying relatively close to the surface. Of course, if you splash a big lure down some distance away from a fish on a shallow shelf it may draw it to the lure, but as you usually don't know where the fish is lying across the river, why take the chance of spooking it? You can always cover the same water again with a splashier lure if you think it might draw a fish.

A small but compact diving jerkbait gives the most accurate long-range cast with the minimum splash, and if accuracy is not too vital then a spoon might do it. A compact topwater lure like a stick bait would easily get the distance but its presentation would only be of any value whilst it was over the shelf. And stick baits are not great for hooking pike even if they do raise a lot of them. If distance was a real problem I would focus on choosing a lure that would reach where I want to be and fishing just that area as well as I could. The deep water between the shelves is unlikely to produce a fish to a very shallow-running lure so you could just work the lure properly until it cleared the far bank ledge then crank it in quickly until it reached the near ledge before starting the proper retrieve again. There's no sense in wasting time working a lure where the probability of a take is very low when you have more likely water to cover. It's easy to get wrapped up in watching the lure and just enjoying how it looks as you work it. But that's the equivalent of a lure angler's 'industrial disease' – playing with lures instead of keeping focus on the fish.

If the far ledge is not too far away you may be able to reach it with any number of lures, so what would be a smart choice? Being in tight control as soon as the lure splashes down is very important and more difficult at long range, so a lure that you can cast tidily is a good idea. It's annoying to be caught out by a momentary tangle on the reel as a fish hits but doesn't stick because you can't strike. The actual depth over the shelf is important too – a fast sinking lure is unlikely to be a smart choice because at range you won't be able to keep a high enough line angle to stop it sinking and fouling up. However, if you do have enough depth, then a fast-sinking lure is sometimes not such a bad idea because it will get to the depth you want before any heavy flow down the main channel drags the lure out of the fishing zone. You might be able to achieve the same objective with a buoyant deep-diving crankbait as well, where the big action would be strong enough to hold it in place.

Lure control

This section moves on to looking at what lure control means when you're out on the water. It should be obvious by now that it is all about the underwater shape and dimensions of the piece of water that you are fishing. Knowing how deep the water is, where the depth changes are, and the position and size of snags – all very basic information but absolutely essential if you plan to fish the spot properly. If you have a boat and sonar then you have a huge advantage over the bank angler – the magic screen will tell you everything. But if you are fishing from the bank you have to use your lures as you fish to teach yourself about the underwater features. This certainly slows down your fishing but you don't have to relearn this stuff on every visit. Your next visit to the swim should be easy. That is, if you took the trouble to remember the important details about it in the first place! Already, after only looking at the far shelf (which is a relatively small part of the swim), you can see that there are a lot of details to consider – and if you ignore them you are not fishing effectively.

Now let's move onto the next feature – the far bank drop-off. The steepness of this depth change is important, actually far more important than how big a depth change it is. The steeper it is, the more fish there are likely to use it and hold close to it, but again there is the context to consider. The more steep drop-offs there are, then the less important any single one of them is likely to be, although if you find one in an area a long way from any others, then that is likely to be very important – even more so if there is a nice not-too-shallow weedy ledge sitting on top of it. It may sound a little inexact to keep referring to 'deep' and 'shallow' without putting any numbers to those descriptions, but it is deliberate.

On my local rivers, the 'shallow' marginal shelf might drop-off at anything from 4 ft to 11 ft and the 'deep' water immediately beyond the drop-off might be between 9 ft and 16 ft. A narrowboat canal might have deep water in the boat channel of only 3 ft with the marginal shelf hardly definable as a shelf at all. This shelf may be only 1 ft deep and sloping away to the boat channel with nothing definable as a 'drop-off' apart from concrete or masonry structures around the locks. Deep glacial lakes, on the other hand, might have a marginal ledge that is 25 ft deep with a drop-off down to 100 ft or more. And on a gravel pit the depths are often very higgledy-piggledy, reflecting the way they were dug. There are more often shallow spits rather than shelves, so defining what is deep and what is shallow becomes very complicated and you have to decide as you go along. It is often only in relation to the nearest water of a different depth that you can call a spot shallow or deep, and that difference is what is important. To be at one depth or another is a choice that fish make – sometimes the choice is predictable and sometimes a surprise, so you need to have tools and techniques at your disposal to check wherever they might be.

Pike, perch and zander love drop-offs and can be found at any point down the slope from the edge of the shelf to the bottom of the main channel. In a boat, the simple way to fish drop-offs is to troll along them or to anchor and cast along them. But from a far bank cast you are always going to be pulling your lure away from the key spot as you retrieve.

'On the drop' technique

The most successful way to fish drop-offs that slope down towards you is 'on the drop' – using a sinking lure that you let fall down either bumping the slope or freely falling as close as you can get to it. This 'free fall' is done under control with a tight line – you want the fish to hook themselves against the rod if they hit. You have an important choice to make here about where you want the lure to splash down – do you want to try to cover the shelf as well? If you have a lure that you can control on the shelf – that is one that does not sink too quickly – you might as well work it across the shelf and let it fall when you judge it has reached the drop-off. (You could soon find this and memorise its distance from the far bank by using the count-back technique.) But if the shelf has a lot of weed or submerged snags it is smarter to aim the cast roughly to where you think the drop-off is. If you cast a bit too far it is obvious because the lure doesn't sink as deep as expected, but if you can just 'trip' the ledge with the lure you know it's right on the money.

As mentioned, controlling the fall is very important, so that you know if a fish hits it. There is another point to consider and that is the trajectory of the falling lure. If the line is tight as soon as the lure hits the water then the lure will fall in an arc and swing further away from the drop-off the deeper it sinks On a sloping drop-off this is not a bad thing, because the lure will follow the slope to some extent. If it is a gentle slope you will have to do a 'lift and drop' or perhaps a series of them to let the lure continue its fall. But if it is a vertical or near-vertical drop then you will have to adjust the technique to keep the lure tight to it. There are a few ways to do this, each having advantages and disadvantages.

The method that gives the most perfect control involves keeping the rod tip high as the lure splashes and then pushing it forward to horizontal as the lure sinks. This works pretty well on a fairly short drop of, for instance, no more than 8 ft. The longer the rod you are using, the longer the drop you can keep vertical. The disadvantage is the relatively short drop that you can manage and the awkward first few feet of the drop when the rod tip is high and a good strike would not be easy.

The second way is to allow the lure to fall with the line slack for a few seconds after the splash and then tighten up with the rod tip high and then lower it as above. This does allow you to keep in good contact at a greater depth, but the first part of the fall is not under control.

The final method is to release line in stages as the lure sinks, adjusting the rod angle as you go. This in theory could allow you to keep the lure reasonably tight to the drop-off and under 90 per cent control in terms of being able to strike – but it's far more difficult to achieve than the first two methods.

Water clarity

The on-the-drop technique will not catch fish if they can't see the lure, so water clarity is important. The clearer it is, the more likely you are to get a take. Once surface visibility drops below 10 in it's hardly worth doing in water more than say 6 ft deep.

Water clarity has another impact, too – the dirtier the water the more casts you have to make to cover it, because the fish cannot see your lure unless they are close enough to it. So with good clarity you can space your casts out at, say, 3 ft as you cover the length of the drop-off – but with lesser visibility it is necessary to close the gaps between splashes to half that or less. Lower light levels also mean you should make more tightly-spaced casts to give the fish a better chance of seeing your lure.

Lure choice for 'on the drop' fishing is basically, anything that sinks at a sensible speed. Fishing across a heavy flow, or even in a very strong wind, can make a slow-sinking lure difficult to stay in touch with, so sometimes you have to use a faster sinking lure than might be ideal. In any case, a really slow sinker is not a lure that will be taken very often on the drop (or at least that is my experience). I suppose though that I wouldn't be using a slow sinker for the job anyway because it requires such a lot of casts to cover the drop-off, and time pressure rules this out. I can't remember having many slow-sinking lures being taken on the drop, apart from during the first couple of seconds after the splashdown. Your lure type is more likely to be dictated by snags than anything. A spoon is a great drop lure, but the treble will find every stick or weed, so while it might be useful casting to a dock side or lock wall, it's a poor choice if you are going to be clipping the drop-off weeds. A jig is always useful to fish on the drop, and cheap enough to lose without too much pain if you get one stuck. You should carry a few jig-heads of different weights so you can select one perfect for the drop speed you want. Spinnerbaits though, are the top choice if it's pike you are seeking. You can usually risk them up on the shelf as well, but you definitely need the stinger hook, and sometimes when fishing them on the drop, the pike hit the blade so you might not get a good hook hold. My first ever Avon double-figure pike came when I cast a spinnerbait onto a narrow far bank shelf tight to a fishing platform, retrieved it a couple of yards, then let it fall down the drop-off – the take came a couple of seconds after the fall started.

Another way to fish the drop-off is with a deep-diving crankbait. Cast it up well back onto the far shelf and begin a slow rod-high retrieve. Then when you judge it to be getting close to the drop-off, sink the tip of the rod a couple of feet or more under the surface and crank hard to get the lure to dive sharply so it goes over the edge of the shelf as it goes down. Then pause and let it rise – a less buoyant lure is best because you want a slow rise that will keep that lure close to the edge of the shelf for as long as possible. The shelf edge is one of the places you are most likely to get a take from either a solo pike or one that is part of a gang, so you have to give it proper attention. You'll never know if the pike was on the shelf looking out or just down the drop-off looking up, but that doesn't matter – it's an effective presentation that should get you some fish quite regularly. The rest of the retrieve over the deep water might be a waste of time unless it is shallow enough for you to keep the lure near the bottom. This is a fairly intense technique, worth trying on a known good swim but rather hard work to use for long.

Fishing the structure – the central channel

Now let's move to central channel. All those sinking lures we used to fish 'on the drop' can be used to fish close to the bottom of this deeper water. (Although a spoon can be a tricky beast to keep down deep and the treble hook will catch on anything it brushes.) Really I can't imagine anyone going out just to fish the far drop-off with a sinking lure and then not fishing across the main bed as well, because it's all part of the same cast and retrieve – unless the main bed was very snaggy or there was a lot of weed immediately in front of the angler.

Simply judging the speed to keep the lure at the right depth is all that is required. A take might come anywhere across the channel, but it is most likely to come from close to a drop-off or submerged snag.

Dealing with snags

Snags are the bane of the lure angler because we often lose our lures when they run into them, and we'd all like never to hook one again. Yet we also know that they are caused by features that will often hold fish, so we have to live dangerously and get our lures close to them. The best you can do is to memorise their positions and take note of the ones that most often hold fish. Some snags are great fish-holders but many are not, and there's no need to risk lures around the barren ones. Snags change over time, they grow and they shrink as new debris is added or old stuff subtracted every time the river rises, I remember the big summer flood of July 2007 which left every snag on the Severn festooned with weed that had been torn from the shallows. It made fishing close to them a constant struggle, and I spent more time cleaning the jigs than I did fishing. From the bank one of the best lures to use to probe around snags is a deep-diving buoyant crankbait – the big lip does keep the hooks away from a lot of trouble. You do have to go gently though or you might jam that big lip under a branch where your only chance of freeing it would be to cross the river and pull from the other side. There's no need to get into the snag with your lure, because only tiddlers hide inside them – it's the fish around the snag hunting the tiddlers that you want to catch. Sometimes, though, touching the snag with your lure is the only sure way of knowing you are close to it.

To avoid snagging-up you have to fish carefully and remember the position of the snag accurately. But you also need to remember your position on the bank – you can often find a mark on the far bank to use as a guide or mark. Be aware that the target mark won't be of any help if you move a couple of yards away from your usual casting position.

A small drop-off in the middle of the river can be a tease. You'll never find it casting from the bank unless it is a very big step – although you might get an inkling there is something there because at a certain point in the retrieve deep across the main channel you pick up fish regularly. A mystery fish holding spot is nice to locate anyway, with or without a discernible feature to explain it. So if you find one give it plenty of attention, make sure you know exactly where the takes are coming from, and never fish nearby without putting a lure right through it. Even with the sonar, those little drop-offs have to be searched for by making zigzags along the river. I still find a new one from time to time that I haven't spotted before in eleven years and thousands of hours on the same few miles of river. They are often quite small, maybe just a step of a foot or so, but despite that they can be very important routes for predators, especially zander. As with the main drop-off, you often find that sunken branches have caught up along them and these snags are staging points where fish frequently rest. These features require no special presentations – the sinking lures used for the bed of the main channel will do the job.

Fishing the structure – near shelf and drop-off

As we get our lure back closer to our bank, we are going to run into the near bank drop-off. This is a hazardous place for lures, because here we will be pulling our precious bait into trouble. As we try to bring the lure up the slope it is going to find every tiny thing possible to hook into or get wedged in, so you've got to go carefully. The near bank drop-off is always going to be there so there's no excuse for repeatedly getting your lure stuck in it – you should be controlling it to avoid the problem. With a sinking lure this means lifting the rod tip and slightly accelerating it to generate some lift: if you get the timing right the lure will come up over the near shelf cleanly. Right away it should be obvious that the bottom of the near drop-off is not being covered by the lure, and there's not a fat lot you can do about that with a sinking lure. If the slope of the drop-off is gentle you should be able to work a jig up it reasonably well, but if it's steep, or if the near shelf goes out a long way, then it will be a hazard best avoided. I hate having to leave any little corner of water uncovered but I know that this is just one of the many limitations imposed by fishing from the bank.

Despite this problem, we still have to give any fish at the bottom of that near-bank drop-off the chance to see a lure. The actual shape of the drop-off and its distance from our feet will dictate what we can do. If, for example, it's a 20 ft wide, 2 ft deep ledge, with a 15 ft vertical drop-off, then we are not going be able to do a lot. But if that 2 ft deep shelf has a solid bed then you could wade out to get closer to the drop-off. However, wading so close to deep water is obviously dangerous, so go carefully, use a wading stick and wear a flotation aid because no fish is worth drowning for. Also you could tie yourself with a line to something solid on the bank so you could pull yourself back in if your feet get stuck in mud. Probably best of all though is find somewhere else to fish, or get afloat – then there are no hiding places for the fish!

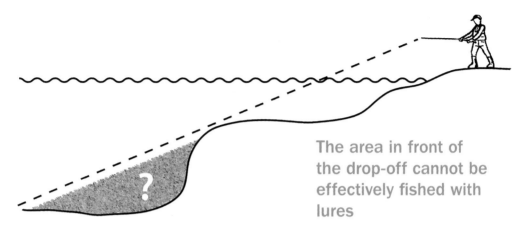

The area in front of the drop-off cannot be effectively fished with lures

Figure 2   A steep near-bank drop-off at the end of a marginal shelf presents a problem to the lure angler on the bank. If you let a sinking lure drop into the blind zone then you risk snagging it as you try to get it up the slope. You have to accept that if this drop-off is steep you cannot fish this important piece of water effectively from that bank.

Without taking it to extremes, a limited amount of wading is often possible and quite helpful. A longer rod will also help you get closer to that drop-off. A near-neutral buoyancy crankbait can also work well – pause it as it comes close to the drop-off and let it hang there, at least it's then giving a fish time to see it and to move for it.

I remember once on the weir pool at Wyre on the Avon getting my deep-diving crankbait very firmly stuck in the clay of the drop-off on one rather over-enthusiastic retrieve. Clay is horrible stuff for grabbing lures and this really felt jammed in. I hoped that if I just let the line go slack it might float out of it as the current tugged on the line. In fact it came out rather quickly, because a pike had grabbed it and kindly pulled it out for me! A bit of a bonus fish and a pointer both to how important that near drop-off is and how just getting a lure into the right place is a lot more important than what it might be doing when it gets there. I didn't have the courage to repeat the presentation though, because I'd lost too many lures there before.

Casting diagonally across the river means that on a routine retrieve the lure does spend the maximum time possible in that narrow band at the top of the drop-off. It really is an important spot where you will get many takes, so everything that might help is worth trying there.

When the near-bank drop-off is tight to the bank and there is no near-bank shelf, you should be able to fish it quite effectively. With the sinking lure that you used across the bottom of the main channel, simply bring it to the bottom of the drop-off and slowly lift it. It's a good idea to give it a few gentle up-and-down jigs while it is still at the bottom of the slope and then add another pause or two as you lift it, and, of course, make the 'killer pause' just before it comes into view. You may perhaps sometimes be able to cast parallel with the bank and bring the lure back tight to the slope. This is always a smart plan, and it's a pity that there are not more places where it can be applied.

All these tactics can work at times, but even with every trick of the trade, it will always be a problem to get good coverage of the near-bank drop-off.

Now let us get up onto the near shelf itself. If you cast right across the river, it is the last place your lure comes to, but it should really be the first place you check out before hurling your lures to the far bank. There just might be the biggest pike in the river a few feet from where you are standing. It would be obviously smart to try to catch it first, before you perhaps land a smaller fish that you've hooked further out or have to drag in a big branch that you snagged out in the river. Big pike don't get big by being stupid and that cautious old lady a few feet from you is likely to move off fairly quickly if she is disturbed by your carelessness. The smart approach is to stand a yard or two back from your normal casting position and cast no further than the edge of the shelf. If it is a wide shelf then you are still taking a risk that you'll hook a jack out there and have to splash it in over the trophy. Also beware of the long fishing platform – it is tempting to race out to the end of the platform or boat pontoon to get to a great all-around casting position, but also amazing how many times you do that only to have a pike take a lure just as you lift it for a recast. Wise up! There are often fish hiding under the platform – pike and perch love these spots so make a few casts along the platform before you go trampling along it. It makes so much more sense to catch the closest fish first.

On these near-bank shallows, use a light lure and a soft cast that lands with a gentle plop as opposed to a house brick's splash. There is nothing more appealing to pike, that are on the lookout for prey fish breaking the surface taking floating insects in the shallows, than that soft plop. As the prey fish takes the insect and turns back down, that pike is ready, and that first second after the splash is so often the key moment, so you had better be ready too. I remember a long time ago on the River Teme that landing a spinnerbait actually in the grass on the far bank and then slowly dragging it back so it fell very gently into the water was far more successful than simply splashing it down tight to the bank.

Weed

If you have an area of broken weed on your shelf, or perhaps a fallen branch, then be prepared to make a series of casts plopping the lure down gently and covering the whole area. The vital part of this is the splash and fall, not the main retrieve. Often enough the first retrieve alongside some weed or fallen branch produces a take and it's tempting to think that one or two blank retrieves is enough and you can move on, but it's not always the case. Meticulously plopping a series of casts down at one foot intervals will often find a fish that needed the lure in exactly the right place before it would move to take it. And the more complicated the shape of your space the more casts you might have to make. You have to be methodical and not leave any gaps where a fish might be waiting. I sometimes think that pike tuck themselves into a snug little spot and are reluctant to break cover unless they are certain of a kill. I've made this work quite a few times when fishing with a boat partner who has had a couple of casts into a promising looking gap like between branches. When they've turned away and decided to cast elsewhere I've made a precise series of casts over their previous spot and pulled out a good fish. In situations like this when I'm fishing along a well-known bank, I watch where my boat partners cast. Very often the first lure through a spot does the trick but if they turn away fishless I will have noted where they've cast and make sure my lure covers the gaps they've left. Of course this multiple splash presentation requires pin-point accuracy, but it is at close range so that's not too difficult.

Bank access

Bank access is always limited to some extent, so getting your lures into all the potential places is impossible, and there are plenty of great looking spots you will never be able to reach. If it's any consolation, I can tell you from experience – after getting a boat and having unlimited access to all these spots – that there are no more fish in these inaccessible spots than on the ones you can get to easily. Clambering down steep banks and beating your way through nettles and brambles to make a few more casts seldom pays off.

Sometimes repeatedly splashing a lure down in one spot will pull a pike from water that you cannot reach. The water has to be clear enough for the pike to be willing to move (getting on for a couple of feet of surface visibility on my usual waters) and you have to be patient, very patient sometimes. Occasionally when I use the repeated splash down method I get a take on the fifth cast, but that's unusually quick, it's often more like after twenty or thirty casts, and that feels like a lot when you're doing it. I suppose the number of casts depends on how far away the pike is and how quickly it moves to investigate the splashing. Unfortunately the vast majority of times I've tried the method it has failed completely, so you might have to commit a lot of time and effort to a plan that is not going to work. It's a low percentage approach, that's only really worth trying when your access is very limited and you have the time to try it. The one river where I've used it most is on the little River Teme which has very steep banks with few fishing positions along some stretches and a lot of overhanging trees in the way. There's a lot of walking per fish so making the absolute most of the limited opportunities is important.

A thing to remember is that if you stand on the bank casting for long enough, eventually a fish is going to come by. So it's important you make sure that on every single one of those casts you retrieve properly and maintain concentration. It is very deflating to put in twenty minutes of repetitive casting and then to forget the killer pause and miss the big pike that has eventually followed the lure in. Before you ask, yes, I have done that.

Open water

There is still one part of the swim we haven't considered and that is the open water well above the bed of main channel. This can often be quite barren, and it's certainly not a place to find fish in very poor water clarity – yet it is the part of the swim that will provide some of your very best pike fishing sessions. It does depend on water clarity, because it depends upon bait-fish being tightly shoaled and the pike being able to see them. Everyone I talk to about this seems to assume that the pike, which has eyes set high on its head, will be deeper than the prey fish, looking up at them. It isn't the case, though – the pike are almost always sitting in mid-water, level with the top of the mass of bait-fish. I sometimes see this on the sonar, and the first time I saw it was quite a revelation and it totally transformed my fishing. Wherever the pike are they usually respond readily to a lure fished somewhere above the top of the prey fish mass. It seems that the pike are sitting around the periphery of the shoal just waiting for one of those roach or whatever to show itself against a background that doesn't consist entirely of other roach.

Simple presentations with big lures usually work – have a look at the chapter, 'Bagging-up', for details.

Apart from pike, there are unlikely to be many other fish high up in this open water. An occasional cruising chub maybe, and sometimes a perch chasing its lunch across the surface, but those fish are usually sitting close to the shelf and should really be thought of as sitting on the top edge of the drop-off rather than in open water.

I've tried, in this chapter, to show you how to deal with the different parts of a typical river swim. But of course, in practice, all swims are different and each one has to be considered individually and split into its component parts – each one of which should then be fished with appropriate presentations to match the underwater contours, the clarity and the fish species. You cannot learn everything in a day. Fishing the same places several times over a season builds familiarity, and only after you have found the places where fish are most likely to be can you really learn about the different presentations.

To sum up, control is the key. Every decision you make when you are fishing with lures should be based upon getting your appropriately-sized lure near to your target fish, then mastering its speed and depth. If you are doing that right you'll catch plenty of fish and if you do that often enough, you might be able to make some productive deductions about how lure colours and actions might improve your presentations further.

Remember:

➤ Success is all about understanding the underwater shape and dimensions of the piece of water that you are fishing.

➤ The most successful way to fish far-bank drop-offs is 'on the drop'.

- The clearer the water is, the more likely you are to get a take 'on the drop', but once surface visibility drops below 10 in it's hardly worth doing.

- Fish close-by first, there are often fish right at your feet.

- In clear water, hungry pike are almost always sitting in mid-water, level with the top of the mass of bait-fish.

- If your lure is in the water then you are making a 'presentation'. It is up to you to control that presentation so you can repeat it when it is successful or change it in a logical and controlled way when it fails.

Rods

Rod choice is largely dictated by the weight of lures that you want to cast. The type of rod, whether it is a tip action (fast) or through action (slow) or somewhere in between, will have a bearing on how your lure performs and how easy it is to control. However, if your buddy is catching fish using a faster-actioned rod than you, with a lure you cannot control, then before you race to the tackle shop to buy the same gear just watch him for a while. He might believe that his 'magic power-twitch' is the key to triggering the fish, but you should be smart enough to know that it is all about speed and depth. So consider his overall retrieve speed and the length of the pause on the twitch, then think about your own lures and the capabilities of your rod and see if you can match him. Beside the action of the rod, length can be important, as can the height of the angler holding it, and the thickness of the line and leader. You might find that even if you have the same rod, line and lure you cannot match your buddy's retrieve because you are too short, too tall, not strong enough, too strong, or plain uncomfortable when you try it. So consider the whole presentation and strive to match it with your own gear and style.

When I started lure fishing there were two types of rods available – a light rod for trout, usually about 6 ft to 7 ft long, casting say, ¼ oz to ¾ oz lures, or a heavier salmon rod, usually 9 ft to 10 ft long capable of casting ⅜ oz up to maybe 2 oz. The lighter rod would be built on a soft, through-action blank and would do what it was designed to do reasonably well, but was a lot softer than you'd like. The heavier rod was a nightmare. In order to be able to cast the lighter lures it had to be quite soft in the tip, but to be able to safely cast the heavy lures it also had to be strong. So you ended up with a thick-walled blank which was uncomfortably heavy and too floppy to offer any effective control, and absolutely horrible for lighter work.

You still sometimes see this type of salmon rod, the advice is, don't buy one! A wide casting-weight range on a lure rod means that too many compromises have been made in its design – it does nothing well. There's really no such thing as an 'all-round' lure rod – you have to decide what weights of lures you are going to use and find a rod to match that range as tightly as possible. Only then can you select a rod of the length you prefer, at the price you are prepared to pay. Longer length means extra weight, which means extra tiredness on longer sessions, but you may find some advantages to that extra foot. Bank anglers generally prefer a longer rod which can sometimes enable you to get the rod tip further from the bank to allow you to fish around marginal weed. I wouldn't disagree with this, but having boat-fished with shorter rods I find that when I switch to bank fishing, my boat rods haven't disadvantaged me at all. It does depend on the water you are fishing – weed-fringed margins might make a longer rod useful, while low overhanging trees would make the short rod favourite. As rods get longer they tend to be less crisp in their action and after using fairly fast-actioned rods it is difficult to adjust back to a more 'through' action.

Why are fast action rods more desirable anyway? With modern rod blank technology, it is possible to make a rod that can cast very light lures with nearly all of the action (i.e. the bend) in the top 40% of the rod. Stiff enough to be able to keep control of a lure but also to control a big fish – one that you want to weigh and photograph! Look for a rod with leverage, with a hardly-bending butt and slightly-bending mid-section, to turn that fish away from danger whatever it might be – a sunken or floating branch, a weed-bed, an anchor rope, or a passing boat. The faster you get a fish into the net, the less chance there is of losing it. I've personally always wanted to net and return fish as quickly as possible. The fight is more an irritation – a potential risk of loss after doing all that hard work in location and presentation. I will always use the strongest line and the most powerful rod I can, because lost fish make lousy photos. Remember that catching the maximum number of fish is what this book is about.

Buying a rod is usually a chancy business unless you have had the opportunity to borrow one that worked for you. Half of the ones I've bought in the past have either ended up being used for a completely different purpose for which they were purchased, or been sold or given away (or more often, lent out on a sort of permanent loan).

If you are serious about lure fishing then you need to realise that you cannot buy a 'good' cheap rod, and, as mentioned above, you cannot buy one rod to do all of things you might want to try. Select your weight casting range and length – then pay your money. Rods are large individual purchases, but cheap when compared to a box of lures – paying more means having a better reel seat and handle, and better guides. While neither of these things are likely to be obvious initially, over time poor quality rod furniture will become apparent. The other plus with buying a good quality rod is that if you cannot get on with it you will more readily be able to sell it.

As you become more experienced and proficient you will identify the need for ever more rods to perform specific functions. I think I will still be looking for better rods for doing certain jobs long after I have bought all the lures I'll ever need. If I'm going out for a day mixed lure fishing on my boat I might take as many as seven rods, although four is average.

Reels

Your reels (whether fixed-spool or multiplier) will take a lot of punishment when lure fishing. You are likely to cast and retrieve more times in a day than most live bait anglers do in a year. Your reels cannot last forever and will simply wear out. In the first place, buy good reels. Those with everlasting bale arm springs are a must, and if they have a good roller that collects the braided line (instead of preventing it going into the roller – reel manufacturers please note) your life will be made much easier. For the entire time you're lure fishing you are going to be using that reel – if there is anything about it that you don't like from the start then you have a big problem. If anything doesn't work properly you will be dealing with it constantly – so if you skimp on your reel, you will be forever reminded of your misjudgement! Good reels often come packaged with lubricant and a diagram showing where it should be applied – this is a strong hint that a spot of oil now and then will keep them working properly, so use it.

Picking the right-sized reel is important – it must match the rod you want to use it on. You rarely need a very large reel for freshwater lure fishing although as your line diameter and strength increases so should the size of the reel. A bigger spool allows you to cast thicker line and a bigger handle and stronger mechanism gives you more winching power to land bigger fish. Just as with rods, you cannot have one reel to do all your lure fishing jobs.

The choice between a fixed-spool and a multiplier (or baitcaster) is down to you. For large lures, say 1 oz upwards, choose a multiplier every time. With it you can use seriously strong line (which protects your lures) without compromising on casting range. When I have to, I will sometimes use lures down to around ½ oz with the multiplier, but as someone who grew up with fixed-spool tackle, I will always use a fixed-spool reel for lures below 1 oz if I have the choice. I know there is a fashion towards using small multipliers for light lure work, and I've even heard some anglers claiming that they can cast further or more accurately with a multiplier using tiny lures. I suspect that they haven't had my fixed-spool background – many lure anglers have come to the sport from either a fly-fishing or general predator fishing/carp fishing background, and they have never learned to use a fixed-spool reel properly.

One of the first things I watch when guiding is how the client uses a fixed spool reel, I can instantly tell one who has stick-float fishing experience, because they have tidy reel habits. I have fished with anglers using small multipliers for small lures – trust me, there is nothing that they can do casting and retrieving small lures that I cannot do with a fixed-spool reel, and I can retrieve faster.

Lines

Line these days has to be braid. I have recently had a look at mono again for some techniques because so many North American anglers use it in preference to braid. Assuming that those opinions are honest (and not sponsored) I can only guess that they must be using techniques that I am unfamiliar with for species I've never fished for. Braid is superior in every way to monofilament fishing line for every type of lure fishing that I have ever tried. But there are braids and there are braids. I've used quite a few good brands, and been present when boat partners have had all sorts of problems with some others – so they are definitely not all the same.

The biggest problem is with rating. I have yet to find one that breaks at its stated breaking strain – some are under-rated and some are over-rated. It sometimes seems as if the manufacturer has got mixed up between pounds and kilograms, or just guessed.

As I type this we are into second generation braids. Up until as recently as 2011 I could have confidently said that you can ignore the breaking strain on the spool and just go by the diameter: if it is thicker, then it is stronger. But there are newer braids out now that are stronger for the same diameter and smoother as well. Smoothness and fine diameters mean longer casting, less drag on the spool lip, and less drag in the water thus allowing lures to run deeper. But how fine would you like your line to be? Very thin braids present difficulties in handling. If you get a tangled knot it is impossible to 'read' so you tug and hope. Also, finer line tends to bed into the spool more readily, especially after pulling on a snag and a finer braid is very easily damaged. A very minor abrasion on fine diameter line can reduce its strength by a significant amount, so finer braids are fragile and less resistant to wear. There is a limit to how fine we want braids to be, and you should always be careful when pulling any braid (on a snag, for instance) that you do not hold the line in your bare fingers. It cuts easily and (sometimes unnoticed) into your skin – only later will you feel the soreness – either wear a glove or wrap the braid around something before you start tugging. Never pull on a snag directly from the reel, it will bed the line in tight so your next few casts are very difficult, and it may distort the spool.

Apart from the very thinnest, I've found braid to be quite robust and hard-wearing. The strong braid on two of my pike multipliers was last changed over seven years ago – I cannot detect any reduction in strength although it looks far from new.

Leaders

If you have pike in your waters – even if you are not fishing for pike – then you should protect your lures with a wire leader (or 'trace'). Apart from protecting your lures you are also protecting the pike from swimming away with a lure and trebles in its mouth after it has bitten through your line. The leader wire is currently available in two choices of metal: steel or titanium. And each of these is available in either a multi-strand or single strand (solid wire). Steel is cheaper and easiest to use – I can't remember if anyone made leaders for sale back in 1989, but I've made my own from the start and never bought one.

Before I go any further I should mention something very important about leaders – I have only found one occasion in my 24 years' experience when a wire leader reduced the number of hits I was getting, and that was from very small zander. Chub don't seem to notice wire – perch don't seem to care (although they will sometimes attack the swivel on the leader in preference to the lure). Despite not fishing for salmon, I get a few occasionally that also obviously don't care. Zander from small (rather than very small as noted above) to large are not apparently put off, and pike – well if you don't use wire for pike you will get what you deserve, shame about the pike that you will probably kill though. I do have a few friends who will use a thick fluorocarbon leader for pike – apparently because it never gets all tangled up in pike teeth so hardly ever needs changing. I also have rather more friends who have tried this and enjoyed the longevity of their leaders but they have had a few bite-offs, so they have rejoined the ranks of the sensible and now they use wire again, but titanium rather than steel.

Titanium is more difficult than steel to make leaders with. It will not twist up simply like steel but needs knots that look horrible to me, and any crimps need to be treble-threaded. But it is superb leader material, very rarely takes on a bend after being in a pike's mouth and getting tangled around teeth or the lure. It is a tedious thing to count but I have had over sixty pike on the same leader on many occasions. If I could be bothered to count more carefully, I suspect I've had a few 'hundred pike' (or more accurately 'hundred fish') titanium leaders.

There is no advantage to be gained by using a leader weaker than your line, so be slightly over-strength on the wire. Unfortunately, I don't think that the strengths given on wire leader material is very accurate either, so aim a little bigger than the line and then reduce the wire diameter subsequently if you have no problems (like wire breaking on a snag pull) that suggest the wire is too light.

Titanium wire weighs less than steel, and this can be important. The few extra grams from a steel trace makes a surprising difference to the buoyancy of your lure – if you have got used to either titanium or steel you can have some of your presentations seriously messed up if you change. Also, aim to make all of your leaders (of a given breaking strain) the same length, with swivels and clips of the same weight. This is most important when using lures that are of near-neutral buoyancy.

Swivels, clips, storing leaders, joining braid to leader

Although swivels have traditionally been part of all wire leaders they are not necessary when using braided line. I don't understand why braid doesn't twist up like mono, but it doesn't. In any case I remember getting plenty of twisting with mono despite the swivel on the leader. A lighter option is an oval rig ring used for carp fishing – these come in a few sizes up to around 50 lb test and weigh around 80% less than the equivalent swivel.

Clips come in a few varieties, I like a duo-lock type, but they do vary in quality, even from the same supplier. It is important to check any new batches and discard them (or send them back) if they are unsatisfactory. Although it is often only when you have been fishing with the new clips for a while that you notice something is not quite right, such as they come open a little too easily, or that they are fiddly to close. Incidentally, you certainly do not need or want a swivel on the clip.

Storing leaders can be a pain. To keep them tidy and kink-free, I use an old line spool, stick a loop of wire to the inside of the spool, then clip the leaders on, one by one, in a long chain.

To join your braid to your leader you should use whatever knot is recommended by the braid supplier – there should be information about this on the braid's packaging. Practise tying this knot until you can do it routinely with cold, wet hands on a windy day in poor light. To tidy up the tag end of the knot most anglers use braid scissors, although I use the cutting part of my unhooking pliers because they're always closest to hand. I never use the pliers' blades for cutting wire because it would soon damage their edges.

Nets

For landing your fish you will need a net, make sure it is big enough to land anything you could possibly hook, because it will only be the biggest and most precious fish that you won't be able to land in a smaller net. There are plenty of lure fishing nets around now with varying meshes – the ideal is around a half-inch rubberised mesh. Too big a mesh leads to some nasty messes with rolling pike: too small, leads to time consuming hook tangles. The latest 'rubberised' meshes are nearly hook-proof. Once in a while a small, fine-wired hook will somehow penetrate the fabric, but it is not a regular problem.

I went through a long period of not using a net at all for pike, hand-landing them all, even some quite big ones (20 lbs+). This saves the hassle of untangling the fish from the net if it thrashes about, as they often do when landed quickly on heavy-lure tackle. From a boat it is possible to hand-land all pike, but from the bank it is not. If you are wading it is easy enough, but on a high and slippery winter riverbank you are putting yourself at some risk in scrambling to the water's edge and leaning over the icy water. And once again it will be the biggest fish, the one you want the most, that will cause the biggest problem.

I decided eventually that I would use a net for nearly all pike because you can usually get a lightly-hooked fish into the net more quickly than if you have to take the time to position it correctly at the side of the boat with a consequentially higher chance of losing it. So now, when using heavy-lure tackle, I use a net for any fish that I cannot lift by putting my hand behind its head and gripping from above (usually fish up to around 7 lb or 8 lb). The days of chinning them out with all the risk of getting a treble point in my fingers are over, and now I shudder to think of the chances I took. On lighter tackle I net almost everything that I can't swing in. I remember trying to hand-land a big perch on the Avon once, only when it shook itself free did I realise that I would have liked to have weighed it, and the net was there ready to be used.

When fishing from the bank I don't use an unhooking mat – the fish are unhooked with the mesh of the net still in the water. On a high bank, where you can't reach down to unhook

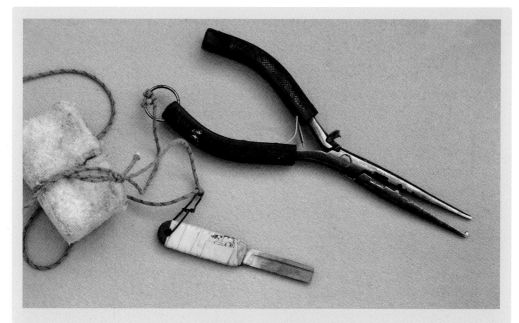

These 8 in long-nosed pliers are just the job for unhooking. They are spring-loaded so it's very easy to get them onto the hook. I use the blades for cutting braid (so I don't use them to cut wire), and they will undo split rings as well. In common with many other lure anglers I have discovered that unhooking pliers invariably sink very quickly when dropped into the water so I keep these attached to a float (some plastic packing foam). I've also got the hook sharpener attached to the same line with yellow tape wrapped around it to make it easier to see. Keep them close by and always return them to their proper place so you can find them quickly. I bet that when you're busy they get dropped and left where they fall so you can get that next cast in quickly. I'll make a special plea here to fishing tool manufacturers: don't make fishing tools out of black steel! Fluorescent yellow/orange would be good, with a large flashing light attached and a siren that sounds whenever you say 'Where are the "bleep-bleep" unhooking pliers?'

the pike in the mesh whilst still in the water, it would be correct to use such a mat if there was no long grass or other soft vegetation to rest the fish and mesh upon. It is something else quite bulky to carry, so I wouldn't take one unless the fishery rules insisted upon using one, or I knew the banks were rough and there was no vegetation.

Pliers and gloves

Essential tools for unhooking fish are long-nosed pliers for bigger hooks. You need a strong grip to free a big hook sometimes, and a good-quality pair of pliers is the right tool.

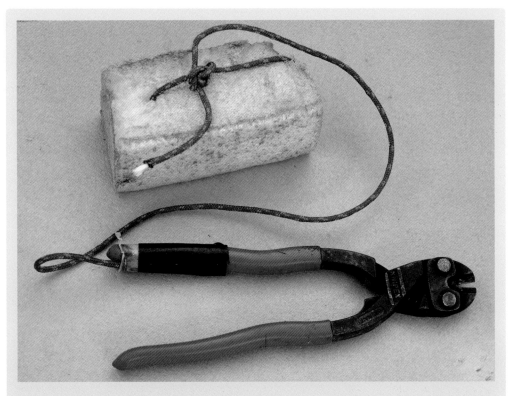

I've had these Knipex 71 31 200 bolt cutters for over 15 years and they've cut countless hooks. They are expensive but they are very durable and they will cut and cut. I know a few lure anglers who think they are too expensive, so they've bought much cheaper cutters from DIY shops. Well so have I – once – and after half a dozen big hooks they were nearing the end of their life. One day that cheap cutter means you are going to have some serious problems unhooking a pike quickly. Note that they also sink, so they have their own float.

For smaller hooks you can often use strong forceps, but I still use pliers, they're just so familiar in my hand and they work quickest for me. Even with small hooks the cutters can be vital, a small perch will sometimes get all three points of a treble in its lips, completely 'stitching-up' its mouth, and sometimes the cutters are the only answer if you're going to avoid some unsightly and unnecessary damage to the fish – and even small fish deserve our respect. While on the subject of hooks, regularly check them for sharpness, watch out for them snubbing their points on rocks, and always carry a hook file to keep them 'sticky' sharp.

Some predator anglers use gloves to protect their hands

when unhooking pike, but I don't, I like to feel what is going on, and have a fear of a treble going through a glove into my flesh, giving me an extra layer of complication in cutting it free.

First-aid

But without gloves you are inevitably going to get a few nicks and scratches on your hands from unhooking pike, and occasionally a puncture from the spiky dorsal fin of a zander or perch, so you need to carry some first aid kit with you. A few plasters and some micro-porous tape will stop you dripping blood all over your rod handle and clothes. Some kitchen roll is also quite useful for wiping away blood, and a lot cleaner than your hand-wiping cloth. I've found that 'spray-on plaster' is really good on 'pike-rash' – those scratches on the back of your fingers caused by the pike's gill rakers – these little scrapes can bleed for ages but a quick spray usually stops them immediately.

Other things I like to have in my first aid kit are Paracetamol and Ibuprofen pain-killers, a few indigestion tablets, some sting-relief spray and antiseptic wipes. Check this kit regularly because all of this stuff deteriorates in a few months – it's very annoying to find the antiseptic wipes are dry and the glue on the tape doesn't stick. These little comforts do not take up much space and they can save you from many irritations.

In the summer remember the sun block. You will fry when you are in your shorts, exposing white thighs to the sun!

Clothing

Clothing shouldn't be that hard to sort out yet I still occasionally get guiding clients without hats or polarised sunglasses. These are important parts of our tackle, you need to be able to see your lure as it comes back to the rod. If you were going away for a week's holiday then you should take spares of each; a sunny day can be badly spoiled when you cannot see properly because of glare. A baseball cap will fit nicely under the hood of your waterproofs, keeping the rain out of your eyes, and off your spectacle lenses.

Your lure fishing clothes will be subject to the same wear as the rest of your tackle – lure fishing is not like sleeping in a bivvy all day! You might have to walk a long way, so you don't want to be too hot. You might have to get through nettles and thorns in the summer, so you need thick material as protection. It will rain sometimes, so you need waterproofs. And your footwear needs some thought, a lot of walking around is going to make Wellington boots or waders very uncomfortable. It may be better to wear good walking boots and carry your waders so you can change into them when necessary. Even from day to day, the weather can vary enough to make yesterday's clothes totally unsuitable, so study the weather forecast and plan accordingly. If you are fishing from a boat you will find it is always colder/windier/wetter than when you are walking the banks, so take extra layers – remember you won't have to carry them.

Camera, scales

If you're like me, you will want to weigh and photograph your better catches, so you have to find room for a camera, scales and a weigh sling. Don't forget to charge the camera batteries, or have some spares with you.

In my experience, how you fish a lure is far more important than the lure itself. Although I've already mentioned quite a few types of lure, I want to give a very elementary description of the basic pros and cons of each. It doesn't take very long on the water to understand the differences between them, and a morning's fishing would teach you more than a book full of descriptions.

Trying to make sense of the all the different classes of lures and the names given to them in different countries, or their different uses is difficult. There is no one correct set of terminology that will suit everyone, so rather than embark on a tedious and pointless attempt to give you my own interpretation I'll simplify the problem, then you can worry about all the different names at your leisure. In my experience, despite all the many types of lures, there are only three important overall categories – lures designed to work on the surface (or 'topwaters'), floating lures designed to fish under the surface that dive when retrieved, and lures that sink.

Topwaters

There are a few different types of topwaters; the two most important for me are crawlers and stick-baits. Crawlers often have some sort of wings sticking out and rock from ride to side creating a lot of splashing. Some are just crankbaits with very small lips that just rock (but do not dive) as they are retrieved. Stick-baits are cleverly-weighted cigar-shape lures made of wood or plastic that can be made to turn or glide from side-to-side on the surface using a 'walk-the-dog' retrieve pattern. They also have the advantage of being great for casting a long distance.

There are two other types that have their uses – prop-baits and poppers. Prop-baits, as their name suggests, have a propeller-type blade at one or both ends which churns up the water as you retrieve. Poppers have a dished face that makes a loud popping sound when you pull them sharply. The important point to note is that the stick baits and poppers will cast furthest.

Under the surface

Beyond finding surface weed and showing strength of flow, topwaters do not provide information much about the water. The subsurface types are our 'probes' and the distinction between the two lure types used for subsurface work is very important.

A floater-diver gets deeper the faster you crank it, whilst a sinker gets shallower – so you don't need too many of each to be able to cover a wide range of depths and speeds, especially when you are only dealing with water down to 10 ft deep or so. Now I'm going to have a look at how different lures behave and try to explain in simple terms what they have to offer and how we can use them.

Floater-divers

Probably the easiest lure to learn to use is a floating-diving crankbait. It is essentially a plug with a lip that floats at rest but dives and wobbles when retrieved. You can feel it wobbling through the rod. The faster you retrieve it, the higher the frequency of the wobble. This enables you to control its speed quite easily. Slow wobble = slow speed. Fast wobble = fast speed. If the wobble slows or dies without you lowering your speed then something is impeding it – you have picked something up on the hooks or the lip, a piece of weed, a leaf or some litter. All this is very helpful – the wobble (the action) is far more important in helping us with lure control than it is for 'attracting' fish.

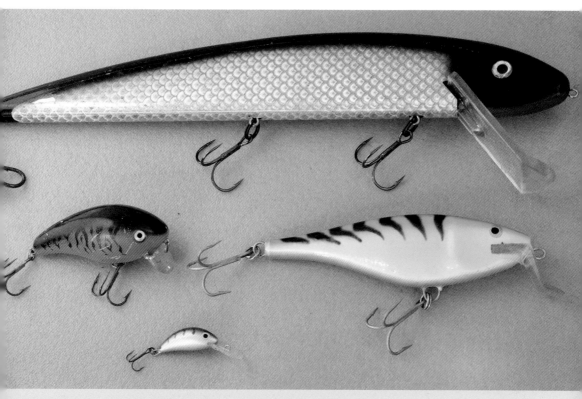

Crankbaits. So called because when you retrieve them all you have to do is to crank the reel handle to give them action. They come in all sizes: the 13 in Grandma at the top is not suitable for casting – its flat shape planes off alarmingly to one side, it looks huge but attracts plenty of attention from pike. The Rapala Super Shad Rap is far more suitable for casting. It is very buoyant though and retrieves at no more than 2 ft down. The Manns 1 Minus is designed to run at no more than 1 ft below the surface – it's on the small side for pike but catches plenty of them, its compact shape making it a good caster and a very useful long-range chub lure. Finally the comparatively tiny Salmo H2S which can only be cast with very light tackle. Such tiny lures will catch small fish of many species. This shallow runner has done nicely for trout and perch.

As you retrieve the crankbait it will dive – just how deeply will depend on several factors. The design of the lure is the first thing to consider, and the obvious thing to notice is the size of the lip. A long diving lip means it is a deep-diving lure, or, more accurately, that it has a steep dive angle. The shape of the lure will have a bearing as well. A slimmer lure will have a tighter action and less resistance to diving so it will get down further than a more bulbous shape. The final factor is not so apparent until you get it into the water and that is the lure's buoyancy. High buoyancy reduces the achievable diving depth.

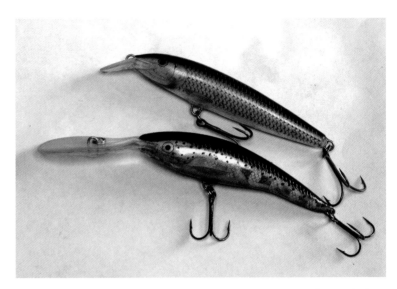

Two similarly-sized lures. Above, a Rapala 14cm Magnum floater, below, a Rapala Deep Tail Dancer. The Deep Tail Dancer's big lip gets it down deep. It will troll to over 20 ft on fine braid whilst the Magnum Floater on the same braid might go down a little over 6 ft. Something you cannot see is the difference in buoyancy. The Deep Tail Dancer will barely float with a wire leader but the Magnum Floater rises quickly when the retrieve stops.

A crankbait with near-neutral buoyancy, even with a relatively small lip, will reach a good depth but the dive angle will be less steep than in one with a big lip. Those features, the size and angle of the lip, the shape of the lure and its buoyancy, determine the crankbait's diving performance.

The effects of speed of retrieve

Now we'll look at your own input. The speed of retrieve is the first and most obvious factor you can contribute to. The faster you go, the deeper the lure will dive (within its design parameters) and the height that you hold the rod tip at will dictate its diving performance. At a fixed speed, you can get the lure to dive deeper as you lower the rod tip. It is almost a direct relationship, raise the rod tip a foot and you raise the lure a foot, but consider, other factors will affect that relationship,

Long-lipped crankbaits get down deep to where the zander live. Catching zander on cast crankbaits is really satisfying because you can get great control and it really feels like you are making the takes happen.

such as how much line you have out. Line diameter is also important, thicker line creates more resistance and reduces the maximum diving depth. This is often barely noticeable when casting, though you will notice it with especially small lures and finer braids. It becomes much more important when trolling from a boat as reducing line diameter allows lures to run deeper.

These factors have to be balanced to give you the depth and speed you want. Every lure has different characteristics, so you have to work out what the depth and speed possibilities are by trial and error. Every crankbait you buy should first and foremost be judged on this depth/speed performance, everything else has to take second place, because this is what really determines how many fish that lure will catch.

There are a couple of other things you need to know about crankbaits before moving on to other lures. You can make the dive angle steeper, thus getting it down faster, by accelerating it hard. This is best done with a low sideways sweep of the rod, but if you have not got room for a sideways sweep because of bank-side foliage, you can push the rod tip deep into the water, kneeling down, if it helps to get the rod tip down a couple of extra feet – and crank hard. These techniques are quite hard work, but worthwhile when extra depth is really important. Finally, it is worth bearing in mind that crankbaits will generally hold their depth with a much slower retrieve speed than that required to get them quickly down to that depth.

Sinking lures

When you are struggling to get your crankbait down to sufficient depth, you are reaching the limits of its usefulness and it is time to consider a sinking lure. You will find that there are very few crankbaits that will get much deeper than about 8 ft, when cast, and a lot of good places on many waters are deeper than that, hence the need for a sinking lure.

Blade baits (spinners and spoons)

Firstly let's consider 'blade baits'. These are lures that have a blade attached, like a spinnerbait or spinner, or a spoon, which is essentially nothing but a blade. When you retrieve a blade bait the blade generates lift – the faster you retrieve, the greater the lift, and the higher in the water your lure runs. The overall weight of the lure combined with the size and shape of the blade will determine its depth/speed characteristics. Given similarly-shaped blades, the greater the surface area of the blade, the more lift it generates, but different blade shapes have different lift characteristics. The broader the blade in relation to its length, the greater the lift it will generate. There are many different types of blades used on in-line spinners or

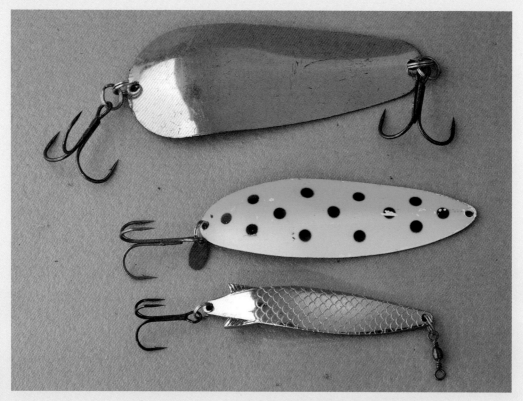

Spoons. The top one is around 5 in long – the extra hook I've rigged on the front tells the story that bigger spoons are not reliable hookers. Sometimes the rear hook doesn't make contact and it's more likely to happen on a bigger fish. In the middle, the Lucky Strike Lizard had been a fair catcher for me but has poor casting accuracy; it is best used down to around 6 ft depth. At the bottom is an Abu Toby – this one I found hanging in a tree on the Severn; notice the swivel which tells me the previous owner was using monofilament line and having problems with line twist, something that doesn't seem to happen when using braid. The narrow blade of the Toby means the lure will run deep and also cast very well.

Spoons are one of the simplest of lures yet I find that they require quite a lot of concentration to keep them running at the right depth and speed. Here I expected to get a few zander by keeping the spoon about 5 ft above the river bed. In clearer water this is sometimes an effective presentation. On an early March day I had this one on the 2nd cast but then no more.

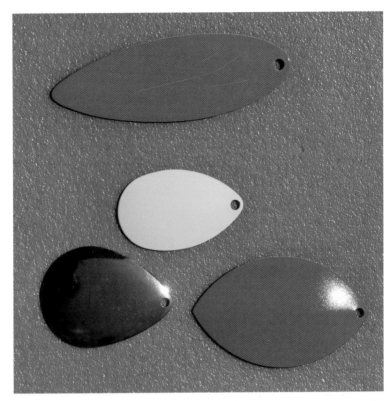

Blades. The 'willow leaf' at the top produces the least lift for its size, the Colorado and Magnum willow leaf at the bottom produce the most lift, and the Indiana in the middle, an intermediate amount of lift. There are other named types as well, with narrow ones providing less lift than wide ones, but blade size is really the most important variable – a bigger blade produces more lift.

spinnerbaits, with a Colorado shape (almost circular) giving the most lift, and a willow leaf (long and thin) giving the least. With spoons exactly the same principle applies. These variations mean that the same weight of lure can have very different depth/speed characteristics.

Spinnerbaits

With spinnerbaits the weight is in the lead head moulded around the hook, with spinners it is in the weights on the shaft, and in spoons the thickness of the metal varies to give different weights. As with crankbaits, the vigour of the action is of far more value to you in controlling the speed of the lure than it

A heavy spinnerbait for casting open water – one of my home-made jobs. It wouldn't win any prizes in a 'prettiest lure' competition but it does the business with pike. This one has a 2 oz head and a big Magnum willow leaf blade. It pulls hard on the rod and retrieves at between 5 and 10 ft at a normal speed. I always make my own spinnerbaits because I've never found any that match my requirements – ball-bearing swivel for the blade, simple wrap-eye for clip attachment which is stronger than a twisted eye, and at least a size 6/0 very sharp single hook (this one has an 8/0 Sakuma Manta) in a fine wire that is replaceable if I have to cut it or it gets damaged by too much sharpening. I've added a stinger hook using a twisted figure-8 connector that I made myself.

is an attractant to fish. You can feel a vigorous action much more easily at slow speed, whilst you will get very tired trying to keep a big-actioned lure moving quickly for long. I do not wish to labour the point, but action catches far more anglers than fish. Just watch a roach or a chub or whatever swimming slowly along – what action does it have? Pike, perch and zander seem perfectly capable of finding and catching them. Severn pike and zander get fat through the winter eating these action-free fish, even when the water clarity is reduced to virtually zero for weeks on end. So concentrate on getting the lure near the fish rather than expecting to attract fish to the lure. It is easy to get carried away by lure manufacturers' claims. They lead you to believe that a lure is just a 'dinner bell' and all you have to do is select the correct dinner bell for the day and fish will be magically drawn to it. They will also try to persuade you that the more different dinner-bells you have, the better your chances of finding the right one for the day. But it's really not like that at all – if you don't put your lures near fish you don't catch any. You can end up with lots of boxes full of expensive 'dinner bells' without understanding why some seem better than others. Its simple – they are better because they are the ones that run at the right speed and depth most of the time.

Sinking jerkbaits

The next type of sinking lure to consider is the sinking jerkbait. There are a great many lures in this genre, but they will usually be gliders or similar – that is they have a side-to-side action of some sort – but there are exceptions. You really cannot tell much about the depth/speed performance of sinking jerkbaits without using them. Their weight is concealed inside them, and just how fast they sink depends on that hidden weight. The vast majority though, are slow, or fairly slow, sinkers, designed to be used in the top 6 ft of water. You have less input on the depth/speed with jerkbaits. They tend to be made to be worked in a certain way, with a certain rod angle and at a certain speed. You can end up buying quite a lot, yet really only cover a very narrow range of depth and speed variation.

Ask around to get an idea of what you are getting before spending a lot of money. Try to match those characteristics to your requirements. They can be expensive, because the best ones are hand-made and the weights are adjusted to account for minor variations in the density of the wood, and a lot of time and skill is required to get consistent performance on a long production run. Cheap copies look the same, but no-one has spent time making any adjustments to allow for the density variations in the wood – so sinkers sometimes float. As always, you get what you pay for.

Jigs and trailers

Finally, the simplest of lures, the jig – which is nothing more than a hook with some lead moulded near the eye. Only in the past decade or so have jigs begun to get the attention that they merit in the United Kingdom. Jigs include all those soft plastic lures with lead heads inside them, like Bull Dawgs, Castaic 'swimbaits', the many small plastic fish copies, etc., but they are all based upon the idea of lead moulded around a hook. The jig is probably the most important lure type of all, because in various weights it can be used to cover all the depths where nothing else can go. If I had to fish with only one lure type, then this would be it, because no matter what the day you can usually find an effective presentation with some sort of jig.

Consider first the basic jig, the jig-head, which comes without any adornment – no plastic or bucktail, just a hook with some lead. There are many different shapes of jig-head, and all have slightly different properties. I say slightly because some of the claims made for different shapes seem a bit fanciful to me. The more important consideration is whether you are going to use them vertically (usually from a boat), just jigging them up and down, or casting them and retrieving them like any other lure. For vertical jigging it is best to have the leader attachment eye on top of the lead head, so the shank of the hook is horizontal as the jig hangs on a vertical line. For casting this arrangement will work well enough, but weed and debris will collect in the angle between the eye and the leader, so one with the eye at the front is better. Some of these types are known as 'swimmer' jigs – but they do not swim much!

Be careful when buying jig-heads and make sure there is a little collar for holding the plastic trailer in place. Some are sold for use with live or dead baits and have no collar, and although you are unlikely to see them in the UK, you may inadvertently order some if shopping online in the USA.

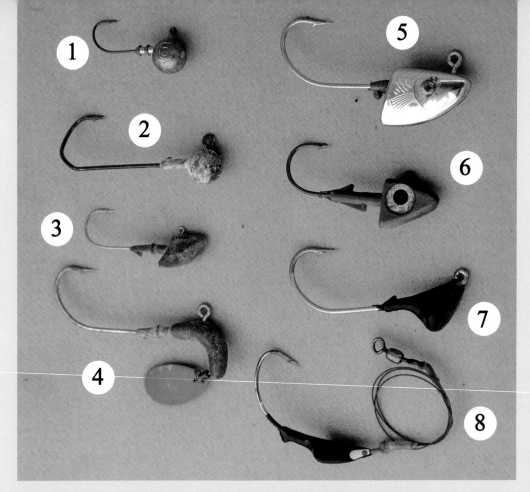

Jig-heads come in many different shapes with many claims made for their different characteristics. The differences in reality are marginal – one ½ oz piece of lead sinks much like any other!

1/2: Round-headed jigs with rather different-sized hooks – the hooks should be matched to the size of the plastic trailer, (1) has a 1/0 short-shank which would do nicely for perch and small zander using a trailer up to no more than 3 ½ in long whilst (2) has a long-shanked 6/0 which would suit a bigger shad intended for pike and big zander.

3: Erie jig – this one holds the hook higher so it is less likely to get caught on the riverbed.

4: Horse-head jig with a spinner blade attached on a swivel – designed for casting, the blade has to be very small or it fouls the body of the trailer. How much value such a tiny blade can have is debatable when compared with a large trailer suitable for such a large hook. The best I can say is that it doesn't appear to put any fish off.

5: A rattling jig-head – this has a metal case with a couple of ball bearings inside, fitted around a lead jig-head.

6: A jig-head shaped to tidily match the front of a plastic shad (as is the rattling head) – it does look less odd, to us, than a round head jig. Quite how much difference such a trivial point would make to a fish I couldn't say, but it does create less drag in the water than the ball-head.

7: Stand-up jig – the flat of the lead is supposed to sit on the riverbed while the body of the trailer sits up enticingly. I suppose if the trailer was small enough or buoyant, it could work like that yet whenever I've looked at one in the shallows the whole thing just lies on its side.

8. Esox Cobra jig-head – these flat heads do sit hook-up, and the short-shanked hook with its exaggerated bend makes it a good choice for working slowly through weed. This one I've rigged with its own leader so the lure clip doesn't catch up on weed.

Soft plastic trailers come in many shapes and sizes. The top one here is a paddle-tail, the one in the middle a split-tail and the bottom one a curl-tail. You will find them described by many other names! The paddle-tail and curl-tail both wriggle as you retrieve them while the split-tail has no built-in action. I would not be able to decide which one is the best fish-catcher. Most anglers choose the high-action options so the split-tail is perhaps less often seen by fish.

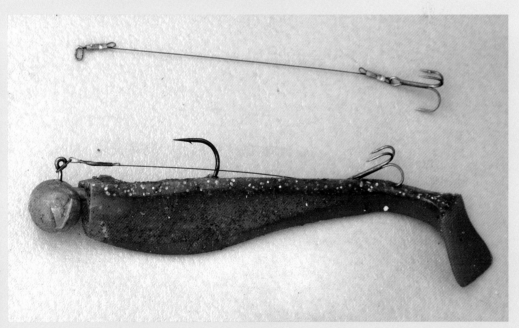

Jig, trailer and stinger on this 6 in Big Hammer paddletail shad. Even with a long-shanked jig hook over 60% of the lure is behind the hook and rigging a stinger solves this. It does not have to be a very big hook. Here it is a size 4 Gamakatsu 13. If I was only targeting zander a size 6 would do. The stinger is a length of wire – in this case titanium single strand of the same 60 lb test as the main leader – with a treble at one end and an oval rig tube at the other that will slip nicely over the jig eye. I always mount my stingers close to the tail of the trailer. I know some anglers would be concerned that this might dampen the action but I cannot prove that this makes any difference to the fish – on the other hand I've loads of evidence to tell me that fish biting on soft plastic where there are no hooks will not be landed.

I remember one day on a big lake where we were slow trolling about 15 ft down. I had five takes and landed three pike on the 10 in Castaic SBT – each of these fish had been just nicked at the very front of their mouths by the rearmost treble that was mounted right back on the tail of the lure. My boat partner had three takes on his more conventionally-rigged SBTs but didn't land any of them. We will never know why fish – pike in particular – all decide on one day that they are only going to bite a certain part of a lure, but it certainly makes our life interesting.

Plastic trailers for use on jig-heads come in a fantastic variety of sizes, shapes and colours. In the murky water that I regularly fish I do not believe that any of the detailed patterns are visible to the fish, but it certainly gives confidence to have something on that looks like a fish or a worm. There are three types of trailer to consider – paddle-tails, curly-tails and straight-tails, I am trying to avoid long lists of lures and their categories, but these three types have many different names according to brand or origin. The paddle-tails are often referred to as shads, and are usually fish-shaped. The curly-tails are sometimes known as worms or twisters, and sometimes have two or more tails as well. The straight-tailed ones can be divided into two main types – those that look a bit like a worm and those that are like a slim fish and sometimes have a split tail. I've used all sorts and caught pike, zander and perch on them regularly – but just about anything with fins will have a bite at a jig and trailer from time to time, so nothing should surprise you. There is a slight difference in performance in that the paddle-tails will sink slightly more slowly than the others because of the drag from the tail, but it is a very slight difference.

As well as the plain jig-heads, you also get those which have a soft plastic body pre-moulded around them, often with extra treble hooks internally wired to the jig-head – the Bull Dawg is the best-known pike-sized example, but there are many others.

Using jigs

You can either cast the jig and let it fall to your chosen depth and then crank it back (note that judgement of speed is much more difficult with these lure types because you get virtually no feedback through the line), or you can allow it to hit the bottom and then retrieve it with lifts of the rod, allowing it to fall back as you take up the slack, lowering the rod for another lift. The lack of feedback also makes it very difficult to tell if you have picked up any weed or suchlike – a sensitive rod and concentration (plus lots of practice) will allow you eventually to feel when bigger pieces of litter are attached, and also when the trailer has wrapped itself partly around any stinger hooks.

The critical matter is the weight of the jig-head – too heavy and it will require a very fast retrieve to keep it above the bottom, too light and it will ride surprisingly high in the water. The key skill is getting the weight just right for the depth and speed required.

Above: Many jigs are available with plastic bodies already moulded around the jig-head. The middle one here has no jig hook and I'm sure some lure anglers would call it a 'swimbait', but it's still a jig! You are stuck with whatever weight the manufacturer has chosen and I generally prefer to have some fine adjustment by being able to swap jig-head weights so I usually use a jig-head and separate trailer. I also like some flexibility about hook size and positioning.

Opposite: You can catch just about anything on a jig. On 6th March 2011 I shared a remarkable session with Neil Roberts. We were fishing for zander and we succeeded in catching 14 of them but the real story was of the four doubles. First I had a serious fright when this 13 lb+ salmon rocketed away, we'd taken a couple of zander from the spot and as this fish took off I thought for a second that it was a pike before the clutch sang out, and carried on singing as the fresh fish headed back towards Greenland. The salmon put up a tremendous fight and I had a great bonus result.

An hour or so later I'm surprised that my clutch is going again, but more slowly, and that fight produced the ugliest carp I have ever seen. It's mouth was very scarred and torn, obviously a refugee from a carp puddle. It was too ugly to photograph or weigh but Neil (who does a fair bit of carp fishing) called it 11 lb+. Later on he had a 13 lb+ pike that we weighed because we were arguing about the weight. Neil was right and I apologised for understating it. Then Neil was in again with this fine 10 lb 4 oz zander. So we shared four doubles of four different species in an 8-hour session – surely a unique event in British freshwater fishing, never mind lure fishing.

General comments and preferences

I have already covered the basic lure types, so before going into more detail about how these lures are applied in real, 'on-the-water' situations, I want to briefly digress from the description of how to use the lures and make some general comments about them. I have caught fish on all types of lures, and I will continue to use any lure that enables me to get some sort of presentation into all the slots that a predatory fish might use, but I do have some opinions about the attractiveness of lure types to pike.

Crankbaits

My long experience of using crankbaits definitely leads me to the conclusion that crankbaits are probably the least attractive of all lure types to decent-sized pike (and I've caught as many pike on crankbaits as I have on probably any other lure). It might be that all crankbaits have a similar movement and that pike learn about them very quickly. So why use them at all? They get used because they are the easiest lure to control in a wide variety of shallow water conditions. It is easy to control depth and speed, so you can at least be sure that you are putting it in the slot. They are especially valuable tools for exploring relatively shallow water (down to 8 ft or so).

Even though some pike might be reluctant to take them, the fact that you will be able to show them to a lot of pike will, to a large extent, compensate. For trolling, the crankbait is by far the easiest lure to use, and they will run deep. There are plenty that can achieve depths of over 20 ft when trolled. The long lip on a deep diver helps to keep it out of snags although it will still find lots of submerged rubbish. Earlier I wrote that too many anglers retrieve all their lures at a similar speed (a sort of medium-slow) and many crankbaits look and feel as if they are working nicely at this speed. To get more takes you have to literally crank that speed up with bursts of faster cranking or rod pulls and pauses. Pauses, like bursts of speed, should be of varied duration, from half a second to as long as it takes for the lure to bob to the surface plus a few more seconds. Up to 10 seconds is not an excessive pause as regards getting a hit, but is rather longer than average, and will slow down your water coverage. It will also, of course, test your patience beyond reason!

Pike sometimes seem capable of watching crankbaits wobble past them all day without responding, but just float that same lure over their heads as slowly as you can and they will not tolerate it. Unfortunately, with a near-static lure you will hook fewer, but at least you have found a fish. In still water you can keep some semblance of a tight line by inching the lure along, but if fished across any sort of flow or breeze it will be almost impossible, unless retrieving directly against that flow or breeze. At the other end of the speed spectrum, you can troll a crankbait very fast and still catch pike, perch and zander. At above 5 mph I find it difficult to control the boat and watch what the lure is doing, but that is not too fast for a pike. As a rule though, I'd consider 4 mph to be pretty quick. By comparison, the fastest you can retrieve a lure with the reel is just over 1 mph, and that is very hard work that no-one can sustain for long, and such work will probably shorten the life of your reel as well.

Spinnerbaits

I believe all the other lure types mentioned are better pike catchers than crankbaits, with Bull Dawgs (and other similar lures) and spinnerbaits being the two most vital ones. Spinnerbaits are the most useful for bank-fishing – you get good feedback from the blade to allow you to judge speed. You can adjust the head weight and blade size or shape to alter the depth/speed ratio – if you only ever used spinnerbaits you would catch pike regularly enough. They work best from just under the surface down to 10 ft depending on the weights and blades. I find they are most useful when fast retrieves are catching.

Jigs

Jigs are at their best from 3 ft down to as deep as you like. But for more depth you need more weight, especially in any flow or in a strong wind that will blow a bow into your line if the jig is too light. As a rough guide, up to about 1 oz for every 10 ft will deal with almost any conditions, but you could use less than half of that if you want to fish more slowly and there are no strong flows or winds to complicate matters.

Spoons

Spoons catch a lot of pike. A long time ago, before the advent of big lures and braid, I used to make my own spoons from copper sheet and fish the Severn from the bank with them. Fishing them deep and slow they were 'never-blank' lures, but it was easy to lose five in a morning in those days before braided line, which was rather off-putting.

Bucktail spinners

In-line bucktail spinners are good for shallow water (down to 5 ft) with nothing too complicated in the flows. They will only work when the shaft is following the trace (rather than when falling like a spinnerbait) so any changes of direction or pauses in the retrieve tend to stop the blade. The best catchers seem to be the biggest ones, and these are usually the ones that present the most difficulties in keeping the blades turning. Despite these limitations in their use they are certainly worth using because they sometimes have a little extra something about them – probably because they might be the biggest thing you can retrieve quickly.

Jerkbaits

The term jerkbait covers a lot of lures, both floater-divers and sinkers. They do all sorts of things, and describing all the actions in detail would be pointless and unhelpful. Essentially you work them with the rod, pulling them and then taking up the slack as they do their thing. They either go down and up, or from side to side, or maybe a bit of both. It is safe to say that they all do something, then stop, and then do something again, then stop, and so on. They all at least have that 'stop' in common – and it is frequently when they stop, that pike hit them. If I could only fish with one sort, then it would be one that I could pull down, and then allow it to rise slowly to the surface, and then pull down again. Like the Musky Mania Weighted Burt, one I use and like. It doesn't 'do' much, it pulls down and maybe a few inches off to one side or the other, and then floats back up – that's it. They are often disparaged by lure anglers who like their lures to wobble a bit. These anglers prefer Squirrely Burts, which have soft plastic curly tails that wriggle reassuringly.

Those with side-to-side actions vary between those that glide and those that just turn (and some that do a bit of both), depending how you work them. They will generally be slow sinkers, but some are made heavy for deeper work and some just float and are designed to be used over shallow weed (the Cobbs Floating Glider is one, the Salmo Floating Slider another). These really do look great to us as they weave their way through the water, and they are great catchers sometimes, but are not as consistent, in my experience, as those that simply go down and up. The points to remember with all jerkbaits (as with all lures) are the distance that they cast, the depth they run at, the speed of the retrieve and their hooking efficiency.

Lure action is very important in respect of lure control in sheer mechanical terms. Action has a bearing on how deep you can run a lure and at what speed, and in pure depth/speed terms, the action is of course vital. At its simplest you will not be able to sustain high-speed retrieves with a big-action lure. As mentioned above, the action also has another vital function: if the lure stops wobbling then it tells you it has picked up some weed or debris – and fish rarely take lures draped in weed. More importantly it will tell you the running depth will have changed as a result of the drag from even a small piece of weed. It's one of the key reasons for using crankbaits to fish close to the bottom or for casting over weed – you know instantly when you are fouled. Some lures are much easier to read than others in this respect, so it is sensible to use those that give the easiest and fastest feedback about this critical detail. The action of a lure, especially the frequency of its oscillation, is also very helpful (especially when you are first trying out a lure) to enable you to judge its speed. Lures that provide very little feedback through the line, like jigs, can prove difficult for beginners to control.

Explore the potentials

A vital point I'd like to make here about lures is that you should fully explore each lure's potential in terms of depth and speed. Later on I'll be writing in detail about fishing in weed beds and weir pools, places where sometimes you have to use a lure in ways that you won't find written in the instructions on the box. Sometimes something that appears plain 'wrong' to our eyes, like a crankbait that is not wobbling, a spinnerbait blade that is not spinning or a glider just cranked straight back, will give you exactly the right presentation. Just keep an open mind about the action and let the fish tell you if the speed and depth are right. Remember that lures are bait and that different lures are used to give us different bait presentations – the more presentations that you can make, the more opportunities you will have to catch fish.

Remember:

- When you use a floater-diver, the wobble (the action) is far more important in helping us with lure control than it is for attracting fish.

- The effects of speed of retrieve – the faster you retrieve the deeper the lure goes.

- Crankbaits are probably the least attractive of all lure types to decent-sized pike.

- Crankbaits get used because they are the easiest lure to control in a wide variety of shallow water conditions.

- You should fully explore each lure's potential in terms of depth and speed.

When you see the heading 'Colour' in a lure fishing book you are usually subjected to a technical and inadequately explained pseudo-scientific account of how light is affected by water and some opinions about how that affects a fish's ability to see lures. If you want to read up about the way light is filtered by water, there are plenty of articles either on the Internet or in the reference sections in libraries. You might also study research on the eyesight of fishes, and may find some reference to pike or other Esocids (especially the North American muskellunge, Esox masquinongy, often referred to as a musky). In a very detailed and scientific way you can read about the different proportions of cone (colour-sensitive) and rod (light-sensitive) cells on a pike's retina, and get a detailed breakdown of the sort of colours they can see best, expressed in the wavelengths of those colours. You will also read that pike have rather less acute colour vision than we have.

You may, from all this wonderful information, be able to devise a perfectly logical, solidly-argued theory about lure colours and their effects on pike. However, inconveniently for you, the pike will constantly ignore your theory, or anyone else's for that matter. The scientific information is of interest – if it's the sort of thing you find interesting – but it will not help you to catch a single pike.

Earlier in this book I wrote that colour was a relatively unimportant part of a lure's attributes. I am certainly not going to expound any scientific theory about how I've come to this conclusion but explain in very simple terms so that you will instantly understand why lure colour choice is not a question that can be answered by simple science.

John Cahill with a small muskie, they are very important sport fish in the northern USA and Southern Canada, so there has been plenty of research done on them over the years. They are quite similar to pike in appearance but their behaviour is very different and they are far more difficult to catch, sometimes called "the fish of ten thousand casts".

What the pike sees

Say you have just caught a couple of nice fish on your 'Fire Tiger' patterned lure, that's good isn't it? Because now you can be sure that they are 'on' Fire Tigers. Really? I don't think so. We do very occasionally see a pike a long time before it takes our lure but generally they suddenly hit and we have no idea where they came from. So consider your two fish (this doesn't just apply to pike) – if one of them was out in open water and spotted the lure heading back to the bank it may well have seen it as a brightly-coloured object against the background of dark. But if the other was near the bank looking out, then it would see the lure as a dark silhouette against a bright sky. Just consider all the other possible variables – light and shade, dark and light backgrounds, water clarity and colour, surface ripple, the constantly changing angle of sunlight and variations in cloud cover. If you could ask a dozen fish what colour the lure was that they took, you could get a different answer from all of them. Also consider how much colour a fish would see if it was looking at a lure from directly behind or in front – all our pretty patterns seem to assume that predators only look at them from the side. In essence the colour the fish sees depends a lot more on where the fish is in relation to the lure than it does on the lure's actual colour. Bear this in mind and you won't get too hung up over colour choices.

Lures are available in a vast range of colours and patterns. Many are very pretty. Many have details like scaled patterns, gills and fins painted on them and they look irresistible to the angler. But what are you looking at? A picture in a magazine or online, the lure in the packet in the shop? Your eyes are about two feet away from the lure (or picture) and you are holding it still in good light. You can examine it at your leisure and see and appreciate every detail. But once in the water, a lot of factors come into play. Like: how far away from the lure is the fish when it decides to take it? How long does the fish have to look at it? Is the lure moving? Is the light perfect? Is the water completely clear? You don't need me to answer these questions, it's obvious that the value of much if not all of the pretty detail on a lure is at best debatable and in reality probably totally meaningless – except that we've been lured to buy and use them, and if we use them we catch fish on them.

Black – a 'magic' colour?

I have experimented with many colours, combinations of colour and patterns over the years, of course, and like all the other lure anglers who have done this (given enough time and experience) I have no answer. A couple of years ago I did some experiments on my computer with imaging software. I drew some rough lure shapes and coloured them in various patterns and colours, pasted them all onto a mottled sort of background, shading from light to dark down the screen. I then put a semi-transparent layer over the top to simulate coloured water, and also darkened and brightened the whole picture to simulate varying light levels. I could be picky and identify one flaw in this experiment – it's impossible to simulate a fluorescent colour on screen (or at least I can't) but I suspect that does not matter too much. Anyway, the result rather shook me. There is one magic colour that stands out against all, but one background – and that colour is black. (An intense bright red is nearly as good.)

But why black? Because black is always black, no matter the light intensity or the water colour, or the background – no matter how it moves against the light. A truly black background would of course hide it, but I cannot think of a single instance of that in any waters I've fished. Light colours tended to show just as paler shapes against a dark background – in the water they can only reflect the colours that are in the water. Patterns only stood out if they were of strong contrast colours (but again, especially black on a bright background). You can take what you will from this – after all, it was only a 'virtual' experiment – but I was fairly convinced.

You could do something similar by looking through tinted opaque glass or maybe a net curtain. Try it at about 4 ft to 6 ft from the lure and see what it looks like. Despite the arbitrary nature of the experiment, you should get a far more accurate idea of what a fish sees if it happens to be stationary and looking at your stationary lure.

What colour to choose?

Where does that leave us? We have to think firstly why we are choosing a particular colour for our lures from the start. I want the fish to see my lure, so that is surely the first criterion. I

I hadn't realised quite how big this Broads pike was going to be when I decided to hand-land it – hooked at maximum range it was very quiet by the time it had fought all the way to the boat.

It was a couple of ounces short of 20 lb but it was nicely hooked so quite easy to chin out.

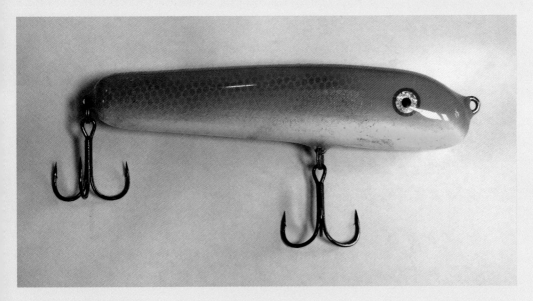

The Cobbs Floating Glider is a very well-made lure with a thick epoxy coating that is bearing up well with just a few scratches to show for a lot of pike action. This bright colour was ideal in the clear water of the shallow Broad because the pike could see it very well and so could I – most of the takes I saw before I felt them when the lure suddenly moved a yard to one side as a pike slammed into it. Brightly-coloured lures are easy for us to see and control in clear water and that's a very good reason to choose them.

would certainly not want an invisible lure (I'd never find it for one thing). Do I want the predator to mistake my lure for a fish? Well, I don't think it would do any harm. But I cannot think of any colour pattern that would make a spinnerbait resemble a fish, and anyway, fish look like they do to make them harder for predators to see, not easier. Might a particular colour scare a predator? It depends how often they have been caught on it, and how well they can see that colour anyway. Pike that have been caught a number of times on lures certainly get harder to catch – but I've no recollection of a day where one colour put all the pike completely off.

To make just one final point about black. In the murky underwater world, with mixed light and clarity, it is hard to imagine that predatory fish spend that much time studying their prey to identify the species or check their colours. Most often the predator will pick its prey out as a silhouette – simply a dark shape – and make its attack. So black is the best colour if you want your lure to be visible as a dark shape.

Very occasionally I've changed lure colour after losing fish because on a lure with several colours the predator might be hitting the lure in the wrong place because it can only see one of the colours. For example, if they are hitting a lure head-on it might be because that colour is near the front of the head. In consequence, you get a vicious take directly against the direction of retrieve, which makes hooking it unlikely. There are all sorts of reasons for losing fish and I bet that the most frequent is the fish grabs the lure in such a way that the hooks do not get inside its mouth. It is worth checking whether a simple colour swap will fix this problem and perhaps it is something to try before you have lost too many fish.

From what you've read so far you'll realise that I do not worry about colour that much. But that's not to say that I haven't worried about it in the past. If you look in my lure boxes you will see a lot of black, silver (nickel/chrome etc.) and fluoro-orange, some dark fish-type patterns, and some white and fluoro-yellow – but I've also got a variety of lures in all sorts of

Tim Maslen with a very pale perch. Fish colours fade as the water gets dirtier. This must offer some advantage in avoiding predation so I like to use lures with a strong dark/light colour contrast when the water clarity is poor. But it doesn't make a huge difference – coloured water simply means that fewer fish can see your lures and if they can't see them they don't bite them. Contrast that with the much brighter perch caught by Artur Brzozowski when the river was a little clearer.

colours. When I try a new lure these days though, I'll usually buy it first in a darkish natural or black and silver if possible but I admit I'm a sucker for an orange belly!

I do pay attention to how pike might be seeing (or not seeing) the lure against certain backgrounds, and might make a change based on my reading of any change in conditions. But it's a rare day when I could honestly say that doing so made a definite difference to my catches. If you're not catching fish, it's usually because there are no predators where you are fishing. Showing different-coloured lures to roach and bream won't make much difference to your results!

Contrast

I like a lure to have some contrast – like dark/light stripes. Nothing too subtle here, it should be bold, because a striped

A Rapala Super Shad Rap with my added 'wound stripe'. When roach fishing you often find that the first fish you catch is injured by a previous encounter with a pike – these fish are hungry, desperate for protein to help the healing process and this makes them less cautious. I guess that pike are used to coming across these wounded fish and being able to take them because they are injured and impaired to some extent and less careful, so it seemed a good idea to imitate that. I've also added a little lead wire here to the front hook shank to reduce its buoyancy. Of course it catches pike, but whether the stripe made any difference I couldn't say. One thing I did notice was how much more visible that stripe was in the water compared to the rest of the lure.

lure is more certain to stand out when it is moving against a varying background. (Note: such a pattern would be less visible in a varying background if the lure were stationary.)

A general rule that works (at least as far as I can tell) is to use a dark lure in dark (i.e. coloured) water, and a bright lure in bright (i.e. clear) water. Fish from clear waters have very clear markings and colours, so I assume that they have some value as camouflage in an environment where they are visible. I notice how fish in my local rivers quickly lose their colours during periods of dirty water, so there must be some advantage to them in being paler then. I think the almost white fish must reflect the colour of the dirty water and become more difficult to see. I've read many times the advice to use brightly coloured lures in dirty water and I think it is wrong. The light colours simply reflect the colour of the water and are lost.

So, under those conditions, I like to make the lure an easy target by making it the darkest silhouette I can. I also like some chrome when the water is dirty. As well as the flash it gives, a chrome lure when seen from below will reflect back the dark colour of the depths, perhaps alternating between flashes of any reflected light from above, which is surely not a bad combination.

Consider also light levels. I am reasonably sure that I do better using lures with some fluoro-orange in clearish water with good sunlight – but it has now become such a standard procedure for me to use them that it may just be a self-fulfilling prophecy.

I'll have to stop here, because I sense I'm becoming as guilty as all the other writers that waste far too much space in discussing colour. If you believe that colour makes a difference then you should change colours often until you find one that works for you. And if changing colours doesn't make a difference then it doesn't matter if you change frequently. This is a win/win situation for lure manufacturers.

The simple answer is not too different from the general message – use what you like then repeat what works.

Remember:

- Colour is relatively unimportant.
- Black is perhaps a better 'colour' than any.
- Contrasting striped lures may stand out better.

What makes a good lure 'good'? I hope I have gone some way towards persuading you that to catch a fish, the lure should be near the fish and travelling at the right speed, and that any lure doing that is a good lure. But there is a little more to it than that. A good lure is the right lure for the circumstances. However, those circumstances – depth, flow, clarity, weed growth, and where the fish need that lure to be before they will take it – vary immensely. As we know, some lures are also much easier to use and control than others, so personal experience and ability does count for a lot in lure choice.

Desirable traits in a lure

There are desirable traits that all lures should share, and we should be aware that there is usually some sort of trade-off between these desirable aspects in order to achieve certain presentations. The one thing not to compromise on is strength – the lure must stay in one piece when you hook a good fish. The hook hangers and leader attachment point must be sturdy. Although the vast majority of lures these days are well made, there are still some that are fragile. You should either not use such lures or rebuild them and fix the problems. Not only is it unethical to leave lures or bits of lures in fish, it is also extremely difficult to weigh and photograph a fish that has escaped!

Strength and durability

Related to sheer pulling strength is the ability of a lure to soak up punishment. Will it keep performing hour after hour and

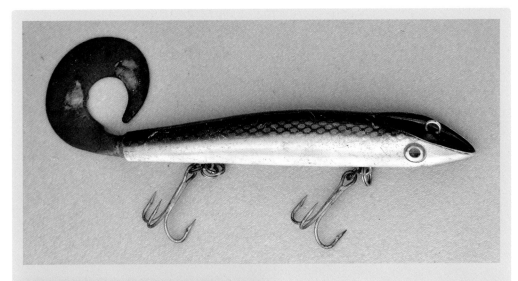

I'm sure many more lure anglers are familiar with the Musky Mania Squirrely Burt, which is just a sawn-off Burt with a soft plastic mag-grub tail glued to it. It looks great in the water and catches loads of pike. But, and it's a big 'but', sawing off the back of the moulded lure has done nothing for its strength and these are devils for leaking after getting a few fish. When they changed the eyes from the old stick-on ones to a push-in teddy bear type they drilled holes to push them into, which created yet another place for water to get in.

They are very good catchers, but so annoying. It would be a great idea to make a wooden copy and be done with all the repair duties. I've replaced the original hooks with a VMC Permasteel pattern – these are corrosion resistant but you can see that after a few months of not being used there is rust on the hooks and the ballast split rings.

fish after fish? Will it continue to run true after some tough work? It's no good if the leader attachment point wobbles so that it needs constant correction. It is no good if the lip bends or breaks. No good if the lure soaks up water or leaks so that the buoyancy changes as the day progresses. Will it be worn out after a few dozen trips? I always choose a hard plastic lure over wood if I have the option, because a moulded, machine-made lure will usually be a more reliable bet. Good, reliable wooden lures are expensive, and no two are quite the same – so if a lure that you have come to rely upon for certain jobs gets irreparably damaged or lost, then you have no exact copy as a spare. Moulded plastic lures do vary to some extent, but generally a lot less than wooden ones.

Castability

Other qualities that vary are casting range, accuracy, hooking efficiency and paint finish. Some lure types cast further and more accurately than others, but even within the different types there are better casters. Range and accuracy do matter, so try to find the best.

Hookability

Some lures hook better than others. You should of course use the best ones you can get. If necessary make modifications to hook hanger positions and hook sizes. Hooks are the key point of contact between you and the fish, so make sure that they are sharp. They come in a large range of shapes, with different ratios between the length of the shank and the gape, and sizes vary according to manufacturer and hook shape.

Changing the hooks on a lure may alter its behaviour if you use replacements that are not the same weight as the originals. Even a slight change in hook weight can change the buoyancy and consequently the running depth. You might therefore suppose that a manufacturer takes a lot of trouble

A Musky Mania Weighted Burt – these are real do-nothing lures. You pull them and they dive, then pause and let them rise, but there's plenty to say about this lure in respect of how sometimes it takes a bit of work to make a lure useful and to maintain it in its useful state. This one's original paintwork was corrupted by contact with other lures – the finish on a lot of the early ones was poor, and this one must be at least 15 years old. I wanted it to imitate small gravel-pit pike which have noticeable bands on them, so I did this rough yellow/green striped pattern and stuck a couple of sparkly eyes on. Notice that it has an extra split ring on the front hanger – this is just ballast to slow the rise.

These lures can vary a bit in performance and they often need a tweak to get them to do exactly what you want. Sometimes that might be just adding a bit of weight, and sometimes it can be trimming the 'face' of the head so that it is symmetrical – if it is not true it will run off to one side and not achieve its full depth. This one is a honey – a couple of slow steady pulls and it is 6 ft down, then it takes over 9 seconds to rise to the surface. It looks horrible in the water because it rises with its tail up at about 25° off vertical, unlike any other lure I've used, and you have to be patient. Takes usually come on the rise, often just under the surface, sometimes after it has broken surface. I've watched a good pike come in close to watch it rise and then oh-so-gently take it after watching it floating nose-down for 5 seconds or more. You have to wait for the pike to make its mind up. This is strictly a clear stillwater presentation for gravel pits and upland lakes.

I've had quite a few nice pike with this lure and they have rarely been less than double figures which makes it a bit special. This presentation is an example of noticing something happen one day by accident – the lure rose up as I was distracted and watching something going on across the pit and a pike took it after it had been floating for a while. I then repeated this to see if it was worth doing it again deliberately. After a few years of paying attention and keeping an open mind you can build a nice repertoire of sneaky lure tricks. This is one of many that I've worked out or been shown.

It's not a very popular lure because it doesn't do much and many lure anglers get bored with it long before they work out its very specialised uses. Another little difficulty with Burts is that they tend to leak after they've caught a few pike and been twisted about in the net. There's not much you can do about it on the water but it's a good idea to inspect them at home between uses and seal any potential gaps in the die-cast seam with epoxy. A final point about the hooks – the tail treble is a nuisance for tangling in nets or catching in the flank of small pike but on this lure the strange way that bigger pike sometimes take it (which is a frequent problem with static presentations) means they get hooked on it quite often so I'd be reluctant to remove it. I wouldn't use this lure for catching smaller pike anyway. I'm sure the little ones aren't so fussy and I could find something else to use so I save this one from damage until I need it to perform its special trick.

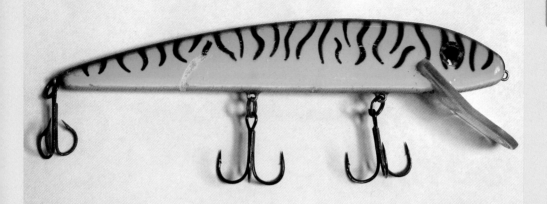

The 9 in Grandma is an easy-to-use crankbait that needs a bit of work before it can be used because it is not waterproof – water gets in very easily around the hook and leader hangers. A few blobs of epoxy seal the holes up effectively. On a hard plastic lure of this length the merits of a tail hook are dubious. With this one I've put a cheap hook on the tail and bent the points in – the weight of the hook is important to the buoyancy of the lure but nine out of ten hooked pike will have that tail treble stuck in their flank somewhere because as you strike it whips around. This modification makes landing and unhooking pike a lot more pleasant as well. I am not aware of any pike failing to be hooked because of that blind treble – even if it does very occasionally cost a fish I'd bet that the extra time it is in the water rather than tangled up in the landing net or slowing down the unhooking process is more than enough compensation.

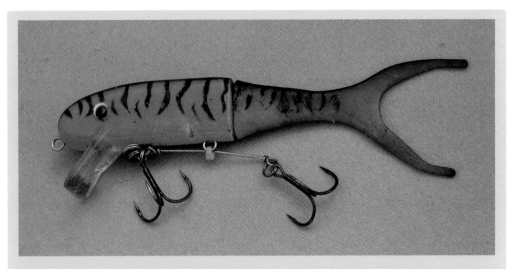

Muskie Innovations Shallow Invader with modified rear hook hanger to get a few points nearer the tail which is where most pike seem to attack it. This is made with a piece of 0.050 in stainless steel wire with a loop and split ring at each end, and a cable tie holding it to the original hook hanger. One curiosity that I've found with this lure is that it really needs 3/0 hooks – they look too big but fitting anything smaller results in an unacceptable percentage of lost fish for me. On this one I've used Owner ST36 hooks. Also notice an extra split ring on the front hook hanger. This is just to add a little weight to reduce buoyancy. Most of my regularly-used lures have some non-standard fittings that I've added to them over the years to make them more closely fit my requirements – that's what makes them good lures for me.

to select hooks that perfectly match the lure, but in 99% of cases you would be wrong. Manufacturers usually select a roughly appropriate size and fit the cheapest they can get hold of. Some lures that I've used over decades have come fitted with different brands and models of hook at different times – sometimes to the detriment of the lures' effectiveness. Too many lure manufacturers don't take enough care over this matter, which is a shame. Recently I bought a large pike lure fitted with two long-shanked trebles that tangled together on every cast, making it useless straight out of the packet. At home I swapped the hooks for shorter-shank ones and instantly fixed the problem, I sometimes wish lures came without hooks or split-rings so I could fit my own. I have boxes full of inappropriate hooks that I've taken off new lures.

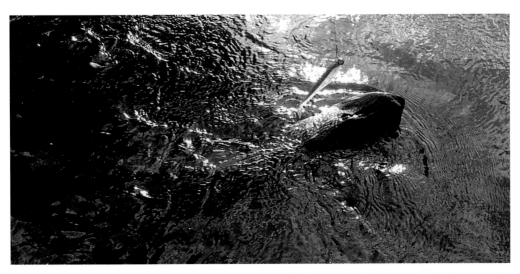

When using larger trailers on jig-heads the stinger hook is important because many fish do not take the main jig hook into their mouths. For zander this is less important, and if a stinger hook is not fitted the lure becomes quite selective in not catching the very smallest ones. However for pike – even decent fish like this 17 lb plus example – fishing without stingers means not hooking about 50% of the takes.

Apart from fixing that annoying tangling problem it is worth checking if the hooks are of the right size, as some misguided manufacturers fit smaller trebles than an experienced pike angler would choose. There is no law saying that all the hooks on a lure must be of the same size or of the same model from the same manufacturer, so if you feel you will get some improvement by fitting, for example, a longer-shank hook on one of the hangers, then do it!

Hooks vary in price and quality. Cheaper hooks can be fine but you have to check quality control – I've bought bags of 50 hooks before to save money and found half a dozen or more that I had to throw away – some with no points, some with broken barbs, some with badly cut points. If you've got time to check through the bag, discard the duff ones and methodically sharpen the others, then go ahead and save the money. These days though I'd rather pay extra for better-quality and leave the manufacturer to sort them out. I prefer a hook with a fine wire and a small barb not set too far back from the point. Fine wire hooks will get damaged more easily though, especially when a big fish shakes its head in the landing net, so always check the hooks carefully after unhooking a netted fish, and have a look at the split rings too. Why use fine wire? Because they penetrate more easily – I'm sure that 90% of fish hook themselves if the trebles are sharp enough and fine enough.

If you want to use thicker-wired hooks then sharpness becomes even more critical – they will only penetrate if they are very sharp. You might think that with a powerful enough rod you could drive in the thicker wire easily enough, but simple common sense indicates that you are just as likely to tear the hooks out of a lightly-hooked fish by excessively violent striking. Whatever hooks you use you must remember that hook maintenance is a constant task – sloppiness costs fish.

Paint finish

The lure's finish sounds fairly trivial, given my already-mentioned disdain for fancy paint jobs, but a good finish indicates in the first place that the manufacturer has taken some care over the lure. Tooth marks are great for inspiring confidence and showing off to your mates, but if you feel that the lure colour and pattern is important, then if it is still the pattern that you bought (or painted yourself) you can retain some consistency in your colour choice. I know I've never seen a lure pattern named 'Tooth-Damaged Fire Tiger with most of the Paint Gone' in a lure catalogue.

Weed avoidance

Weed and snag avoidance vary between lure type and within types. Choose the one that works best for the type of conditions, weed species and snag type (rock or branch) that you have to deal with. It can be quite subtle, but if you are struggling with such problems you should consider how a different lure might do better. It is important once again to

This low double pike is hooked on a Muskie Innovations Bull Dawg with my own hook rigging. It was first devised over ten years ago to reduce snagging which it does very well. Experience has shown other advantages as well. Very often (like here) the body of the Dawg hangs free of the pike's mouth and reduces tooth damage, and without the body in the mouth the pike is a lot easier to unhook. A final plus is that you can use smaller hooks than standard. They come fitted with 3/0 size as standard but changing to 2/0 and then 1/0 (after more experience) has been efficient and that has given even more benefit in snag avoidance and easy unhooking.

ditch your preconceptions about the right lure action, and get something in there that you can fish through, around or over the hazards.

Casting range vs. running depth

The most frequent trade-off in attributes comes between casting range and running depth. A buoyant deep-diving crankbait with its big lip, for example, is never going to be a great caster, but some will be better than others. The other major trade-off is that a lure with great weed avoidance characteristics is probably going to be compromised in its hooking ability. You have to choose lures carefully to deal with these compromises. One of the best reasons for trying new lures is to see if they do offer advantages or different blends of compromise to deal with these questions.

Testing

How long a trial should you give a new lure? Consider one of your 'best' lures, one that you use often in your waters because it covers the depth and speed range that catches some fish for you fairly regularly. You know this is a good catcher, but no matter how many fish you catch with it, even on a great day you will make an awful lot of casts that do not catch any fish. Are you prepared to make at least as many unsuccessful casts with the new one?

There is a real danger when trying a new lure that you will be very suspicious of one that behaves very differently from the lures you normally catch with. Because of this, you give it a trial of a dozen casts or so and then relegate it to the tackle box, often permanently. The end result of such unsuccessful 'trials' is you end up using a very narrow range of lure actions when in fact the widest possible range of performance is desirable. I've heard many anglers praising the action of a particular lure, and read hundreds of descriptions of 'irresistible' lures, and

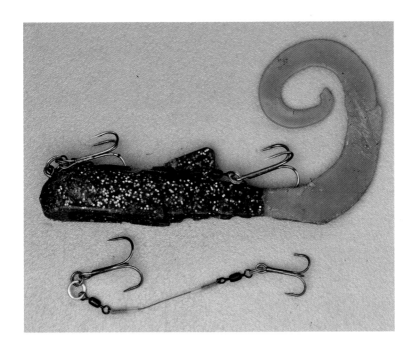

This is a Bull Dawg with my own rigging. I snip off the big jig hook which only gets in the way then make the stinger rig with a big split ring, 100 lb swivel, some 90 lb Marlin 7-strand wire, another swivel and split ring. A short piece of shrink tube over each wire twist is tidy but not essential.

many, many anglers are confident that they know what sort of lure action will appeal to a fish. This is where it is so easy to let some subjective opinion prevent you from using something that you don't like, and be aware, it is only your opinion, not the fish's. One thing I know is that I haven't a clue what action will appeal to a fish any more or less than any other action. Every action is equal, from no action to the most violent, so it is rather like the speed issue, everything works – sometimes.

But first, you should consider why you are trying a new lure. Will it be superior to one of your old regulars in any of the key attributes like casting, strength, durability, weed or snag avoidance and hooking? Having two different lures that do essentially the same job is pointless. I've seen lure boxes crammed with small, shallow diving crankbaits that cover such a small range of options collectively that just a handful of them could cover everything that the whole lot could do.

Try to be logical when assessing the new lure. Start with the basics – is it strong enough? I hope that you would check this before getting it in the water, and fix anything you have any doubts over – replace split rings and hooks if you don't trust them, and sharpen the hooks. You can tell straight away if it is a good caster. I don't think there is much point using a lure that tangles up on one cast in three. I know that tangling lures are usually a result of some fault in casting technique (or occasionally retrieve pattern) and you can of course try to adjust your casting to suit, but if it requires too much effort then it will be a constant source of aggravation.

You can also tell pretty quickly what speed and depth range the trial new lure covers. Test it in a swim you know well, one with a clean bed, with no snags, and depths you already know. This initial test will quickly tell you that it might be usable, and where it might be of value. All you have do then is assess whether the new lure offers any significantly different presentation to those you can achieve with your old lures? If not, then you have to make a call as to why you might prefer it to your existing ones. Compare casting performance, durability and price. We all lose lures from time to time, and it's nice when we can afford the replacements. It's also nice not to be afraid to use them for fear of snagging, so price is another factor in a lure's usability. Beyond the obvious, it can often take quite a while for you to learn everything important about a new lure – you have to give them a fair test.

Be cynical about claims

Every article you ever read will mention some lure or other that you haven't got – and it is tempting, given the ease of obtaining stuff these days via the Internet, to buy them all. You should analyse these articles carefully and try to understand in what context the lure is being used, because a great lure for trolling deep on a Scottish loch is not going to be of much use on your local canal. Tackle choice matters too – lures are only properly usable with the appropriate rods, reel and line, so take care to read what tackle is being used and compare it to your own – casting Bull Dawgs on spinning rods is not recommended. You might also apply a little cynicism to some of the recommendations you see, because some writers get paid by sponsors for mentioning the lures supplied. Think about these things and spend your money wisely. All the lures that I name in these pages are mentioned because they are readily available (as I write) so you may already be familiar with them or can obtain them easily to assess them. They all do what I need them to do – I bought them and use them because of that.

Remember:

- ➤ A good lure is the right lure for the circumstances.
- ➤ Desirable traits in a lure are strength and durability, castability and hookability.
- ➤ It is important to give any new lure you buy a decent trial period.
- ➤ Decide whether the new lure offers any significantly different presentations to those you can achieve with your old lures.

Section Two
STRATEGY

So far this book has dealt with the basic technical side of lure fishing – from now on it deals with the strategy i.e., what happens when you're actually fishing and how to deal with the different situations you encounter. This is what really matters – all the lures in the world are useless without any fish, and knowing how to deal with all the different situations you encounter when you are fishing will keep your lures close to fish. This is all part of that wonderful skill called 'watercraft'.

As I have already mentioned – and will again – the key to success is getting your lure near fish, and the more fish the better. If you maintain good lure control and pay attention to where you are catching your fish then you will, in time, become a consistently successful lure angler. In this part of the book, you can learn how to cut that time down by reading about what time has taught me.

We know that fish like perch and zander live in shoals, and chub we know, are regularly found in numbers in the same swim, but what about pike? How many times have you read that the pike is a 'solitary hunter'? Like me, too many, I bet. Pike fishing literature almost seems to start with this premise – yet it is wrong for much of the time. I know pike are not shoal fish but plenty of live-bait anglers have tales of groups of pike passing through their swims when the rod alarms go off one by one as the fish move along. Pike are not a strictly solitary fish – they often move around together in small groups and are often found together in loose concentrations, sometimes obviously close to shoals of prey fish, but sometimes not. Finding these groups is the key to success with pike – exactly like finding good chub swims, or shoals of perch and zander.

When to fish with lures

Before we start fishing, we should consider whether we should be fishing with lures, or whether baits are the smarter option. This decision is mainly dependent on the numbers of fish present and whether you have good access to them. Knowledge of the water is the key and whilst sometimes you might have to fish it a few times to gain that knowledge, usually there are some clues.

Consider fishing from the bank on a large gravel pit – you will only be able to cover a tiny fraction of the water area with lures, and usually the pike will have learned to be a little wary of coming too close to the bank. This is where you will often see long-range bait tactics like balloons or bait boats being used, and it's an obvious sign that stuck on the bank your chances of success are extremely low.

Another difficult water for lure fishing is an overgrown small river. On such rivers, access points can be few and far between – again you will only be able to cover a fraction of the water and it's likely you'll only get one or two fish from any spot before you've frightened any others away.

Apart from limited access and range you have to consider the fish population density. Lures are most effective when you are able to fish them among lots of competing predators, and in such happy circumstances I'd expect sensibly-fished lures to outfish baits most of the time.

On the other hand, when fish numbers are low, fishing with lures can mean a lot of casting for no reward. That is when a 4-rods and bait approach is the only practical way to fish, waiting for the target predator to come by. Even on quite prolific waters there are times when baits outscore lures, such as when the fish – pike or zander – are moving around rather than sitting on spots. Well-placed baits can intercept every moving fish – but you need a lot of luck to be in the right place at the right time with your lure. I'm not implying that bait fishing is intrinsically better than lure fishing, because I know that is not

When you find a group of pike the action can be fast and furious – on this occasion James Ashworth and I caught 19 pike between us from an area the size of a tennis court. We were getting lots of takes and follows between playing and landing fish so neither of us wanted to stop casting. Finally we had to call a truce so that we could both answer the call of nature and get something to eat! We ended the day with 11 pike each – an unusually fair result.

the case, but that a static presentation will keep the bait in the right place whereas your lure is only ever going to be in any given place for a fraction of the time.

Now to the good times – when lures are better than baits. You can score heavily with lures when your target predators are in packs, and concentrated in holding spots. As you are far more mobile than the bait angler you can check out any such spots far more quickly, and you have a vastly superior armoury of speed and depth presentations. A bait angler will generally invest a lot more time on a spot before deciding that there are no fish there. After all he's had to set up all that gear and if the fish aren't there he has to wait in case they come to him. We lure anglers however are much more pro-active – we can go to the fish!

In weed beds, baits are really difficult to fish, and live-baits practically impossible, yet sensibly-fished lures can work like a dream in some pretty dense underwater foliage. Around sunken trees live-baits are prone to getting themselves tangled, whereas a skilful lure angler can work his lures quite effectively.

The essential key to getting your lures into all these great places is access. On little rivers you might need chest waders, some kit to clear a safe path to the water though the nettles, and maybe a rope to let yourself down a steep bank, but on larger waters the only answer is a boat. Whereas from the bank the bait angler is far better equipped to cover the water, when you get afloat you are on a level playing field, and his four rods are easily matched if the fishery rules allow you to troll (if you have the time to put in to learn this often-misunderstood technique).

Even without trolling, your ability to check any number of spots out quickly is going to give you a huge edge, and although you might have to check out quite a few to find one that has fish, the mobility of the boat means that you can.

I mentioned earlier in this book that lure fishing is a tough discipline and success means putting in a lot of effort. It can be physically demanding too, and I don't blame any angler who decides that he'd rather sit quietly watching 4 floats or indicators than working himself to exhaustion trying to come to terms with lure fishing. But if you're up for the challenge, then here is how to go about it. In essence all fishing with lures can be split into three modes:

· Looking for a concentration of fish (searching).
· Catching those fish when you've found them (bagging-up).
· Doing whatever it takes to catch something when you haven't found such a concentration (scratching).

The details of how different predator fish species behave will vary from water to water, through the seasons of the year, with fluctuations in their populations and those of their prey fish,

This jig-caught fat winter zander weighed over 15 lb. The river was carrying a couple of feet of extra water and we noticed after a couple of hours that the key to getting fish was finding exactly the right flow speed, This sort of observation is far more important than worrying about trivial details of lure choice.

with changes in weather and for other reasons we can only guess at. We know the general principles that govern these fish but the details are beyond our knowledge. We can be sure that they need to eat, breed and find protection from predation themselves, but as soon as we start to speculate beyond these basic needs we are guessing. These guesses might be interesting to read but they won't make any difference to your success – read them and be entertained by all means, but don't go basing any fancy theories and plans on them because they don't stand any examination.

When you become familiar with a particular water, you do start to recognise repeated fish movements related to the seasons, water clarity, weather, and suchlike. Long-term familiarity will also show you that sometimes there are striking exceptions to these basic movements – in some years they simply don't happen. Everyone I know can tell me about some fantastic fishing that they have enjoyed in the past, but 'it's not the same now'. I have some memories like those as well. Really good fishing is often down to unusual conditions that persist for some time, or an unusual sequence of conditions that leads to large concentrations of fish. My advice is to just make the most of them, because you might be old before they happen again. However, in the main, you can make generalisations about fish behaviour and movements after gaining knowledge of a water over a few years – important knowledge, as it can save you a lot of wasted fishing time if you simply know where the fish will not be. So pay attention when you are fishing to the time of year, the water conditions (especially clarity), the weather and anything else that might affect the water. Remember the details and you'll surely have a better chance of repeating successes and avoiding failures.

Remember:

- All the lures in the world are useless without any fish.
- Pike are not a strictly solitary fish, they often move around together in small groups.
- All lure fishing can be split into three modes – searching, bagging-up and scratching.

Familiar waters: Planning

After a few trips to the same venue you should have identified the best places to fish, so on subsequent trips you'll know where to fish and be able to avoid the empty water. You should also, by this time, have a rough plan about the order in which you will fish places. This plan can simply be linear, i.e., taking them in the order you get to them. Or it might be more subtle, in that you may know of perhaps two really good places and maybe half-a-dozen medium-quality spots. Then there are also a few places you know that that turn up fish only in certain conditions, like dirty or clear water, heavy flows or strong winds. Also places you really like the look of, that haven't produced yet but you'd like to try again.

It's key to go to the best places first, because you must spend the most time where you have the best chances of finding some fish. You may have to walk past a few of the medium-quality spots to get to the best places. It makes sense, however, to do so, because if you are going to have a really good session then there is a very high probability that one of your best places is going to turn up fish, and you have to allocate enough time to fish them properly.

However you may have time on the return journey to drop in on the lesser swims and try them. You might also have caught a few fish that give you a clue about which of the lesser swims might give you the best chance of a few fish – swims with, for example, a similar depth or amount of weed as the swims where you caught earlier. One of the lure angler's best weapons is mobility, just remember that being mobile does not mean having to fish miles of empty water, but being able

'Look at that,' said Seb Shelton as the large hump on the riverbed scrolled across the sonar screen. 'I know,' I replied, 'it looks great but it's never produced a fish'. Then my rod went over! That falls into the category of spots that you fancy but with no form – they're worth a cast or two if you're passing.

to visit all the best swims. Keeping your lures as close as you can to the maximum number of fish is the golden rule. If you keep managing this, you will soon work out the presentations that work most often.

In essence, searching known swims for groups of fish is simple enough. You are obviously in a far better position than when searching water you haven't fished before as you have knowledge about what presentations have worked best there before. You know the likeliest depths, and perhaps have identified a particular spot in the swim that usually turns up the most or best fish – but you do have some decisions to make. Such as how long are you going to stay there? A swim you know and have had success fishing before is certainly worth more than just a quick whiz around.

Making best use of time

It is important to have a rough plan in your head. If you have a choice of good swims, it is foolish to spend all day blanking in one without trying another, because even on the best days there are not enough fish to fill every swim.

Time soon ticks away, and if you don't get any action early on to help you out with presentations, you've got to try a few casts in all your good places. You can easily find yourself a long way from your base with darkness closing in, and a long walk or boat trip back. If I plan on fishing any distance from the car, I'd rather get that long trip done first and work my way back as I fish. I like to leave somewhere good close to the car that I'll fish for the last hour or two, so I can spend the last of the daylight fishing instead of travelling. A final note about waters you know well is that you can tailor the lures you pack to match what you know you are going to find. You might not reduce the overall number you carry but you can increase the variations within the depth ranges that you know you will have to fish.

Quite often on a good day you can find some key piece of information early on – like lure retrieve speed – that will work all day. Once you've had that sort of breakthrough, you can to some extent bank on it as the best way to check other swims. You can still try other things, but unless the weather changes very dramatically (especially light levels) then the chances are that the same presentation will work best all day, so that becomes your search presentation, even if it's a slower option than you might normally choose for searching.

Given a number of good swims to try, if you get a good result in one you can expect to get another good result somewhere else, so don't rest on your laurels but keep checking other places. And one particular point to note is that a good catching day is a good day to check water that you fancy that maybe has no form – but don't waste time trying to prove a point, because there's bound to be other fish waiting in your known spots.

New waters: Pre-planning

Say you're on a water for the first time – you know you've got to find some fish, but where do you start? The process begins before you get to the new venue. Hopefully, you have not just pulled the place out of the air – you must already have some information – the species of fish you want to catch, at the very least. If you can make the time it's a good idea to have a walk around the water on a nice Sunday morning when there is a good chance of seeing someone else fishing.

Talking to fellow anglers

Even if they are not fishing for predators you might be able to learn something from them. Something basic, like the depth of the water can save you some trouble later – you won't need any fast-sinking jigs on a 5 ft-deep lake, for instance. If you do talk to a non-predator angler, you have to take their estimations of the size of pike they have seen taking their roach with a certain amount of caution. Every pike is 20 lb, because that's the only number a non-pike angler knows! But at least he won't be cagey about where he has seen pike, or anglers catching them.

On the other hand, a pike angler might be very evasive about what he has caught, perhaps even preferring to tell you about better waters just up the road. If there are a few anglers present, just be friendly and ask, then it is up to you to filter the information and decide what might help you. Stories about the size of fish are of limited value but if you see a fish caught, or even see where any competent-looking predator angler is casting, you have a start.

Talking to another lure angler can be especially helpful ... or not. Lure-angling does appeal to more than its fair share of eccentrics, so you might well find yourself the recipient of a fervent lecture about some trivial aspect of his favourite lure rather than any useful information. I've met some very enthusiastic lure anglers who catch very few fish, but that inconvenient detail does not apparently deter them from passing on their 'wisdom'.

So, information from other anglers on the bank is of limited value – they might be plain bad anglers, or unwilling to encourage anyone else to pressurise 'their' fish. If you can find someone who was a regular on the water at one time but no longer fishes it, they will often be willing to give a lot more away because your presence will not detract from their results. Of course you can also ask in local tackle shops, but you need luck to get any really useful information.

You eventually have to make a start on your own, so how do you go about it?

Focus your search

For you to have a good day you have to find a concentration of fish. It makes no sense just to try every lure in every swim because it takes too long and it is unnecessary in the context of finding a group of fish, as you are relying on these fish to be competing for your lure. So start with a simple presentation that you can cast as far as you need to, and retrieve fairly quickly. You've got to choose at what depth to fish and there are two key ways to think about the depth. How far below the surface or how high above the bed? In very deep water like 15 ft or deeper, I ignore the bottom if searching for pike and only focus on the top 6 ft – especially the foot or so just beneath how far I can see into the water.

For zander it's a case of putting on a heavy jig and retrieving quickly but carefully. For perch, either a smaller version of the zander presentation, or something like a spinner near the surface. You can't try everything if you are looking for a sign of numbers of fish, you have to trust the fish. I don't want to be too dogmatic about what lure you should use, the point is that it should be easy to cast and easy to control at a brisk retrieve speed. You almost have to slip into autopilot so the lure is consistently doing its stuff, while you are dividing your concentration between what the lure is doing and what is going on around you.

Look for clues

If there are obvious clues that there is a better place to try, you don't have to keep searching all the water between you and that place. Get moving if you see someone else catching. Pay attention to anyone shouting to his mate for a net, and look out for camera flashes. Seeing a fish caught is the surest way to identify a good spot, even if you can't fish there now you can see what techniques are being used and what depths the fish are at. Watch out for prey fish obviously being attacked by predators. Perch in particular can be easy to spot as they chase little fish, while pike also show themselves sometimes when attacking their prey close to the surface. Just be careful not to race along casting at every biggish swirl because other large fish like bream and carp also break surface (rather more often than pike) and note that small fish will scatter in panic when any large fish such as a cruising carp comes near.

Change your approach

As soon as you get any sign of a fish in your swim, a take, or perhaps just a follow, you should change your approach. You need to know whether that fish is solo or with company. If you get the fish, then whatever presentation you are using must be right, so stick with that and cover the swim. If there is no immediate further response stick with the same lure and vary the speed and/or depth of the retrieve, as often a fairly simple change will be enough to make other fish respond.

If this doesn't provoke a reaction, try a different presentation. You have one key piece of information – the position of your lure when you made contact with the first fish. This is your starting point, so work around that position, varying speed and depth again – but you are unlikely to have to change radically

Sometimes you feel what you think are hits and you spend time trying to convert them into fish, but beware of bream! Very often the only clue is the slime on the leader but occasionally one of them has a proper go at a lure and manages to get a hook in its mouth.

because if that first fish was part of a group then they will be responding in a similar way. If this produces more fish then of course you've found a group, but a 'group' might only be a couple of fish, so you have achieved the purpose of your search. (Exploiting the opportunity to take as many fish as possible from a group is described in the next chapter.)

Although I think finding these groups of fish is the key to great sport, I am only too well aware that on most days such groups of active fish are not present. There still may be groups, but they are not feeding or perhaps they have broken up.

Revisit structure

If you've been all around your new venue and haven't found a group of fish then what? As you have no information as to what is the best spot there's no reason to spend a lot of time in any one place. But did you see any places that looked more interesting than the main body of water? Here's a tip that's saved me countless fishless days – revisit any structure you've found.

Such as inlets and points, feeder streams, weed beds, sharp depth changes, sunken trees, boat moorings or landing-stages (with or without boats) – anything that has deflected, blocked, speeded up or slowed the main stream. The one feature that all waters share is a bank, and the interface between bank and water is one difference you can always work with.

Weed beds are a special case, and I'll deal with them in a separate chapter. But if you've had no evidence of fish on your search then look again at all the other structure and simply treat it as if you have seen a fish there. If there are plenty of such places you could treat them as if you were searching again – but use a different search presentation to the one you used first time around. Visit every place that you think looks worthy of further examination. If there are only one or two places that look different and interesting then you have to work them thoroughly. This may sound quite a lot like the typical advice given in many predator fishing books, especially for pike, where the 'solitary hunter' lies in wait under a boat or alongside a sunken tree – the difference though is the emphasis I'd give it. This is your second line of attack on a new water when you have failed to find active groups of fish in open water. If you only ever use this approach of trying the places you fancy then you will catch fish often enough, but you will almost certainly miss out on the bumper days when you can catch many nice fish.

Very often, features that hold groups of predators are not visible on the surface – like shoals of prey fish or sharp changes in depth some way from the bank. Quite often there's no notable feature at all, even when you check it thoroughly with a sonar from the boat – the only conclusion to come to, is the fish are there because they just happen to like that spot.

But what happens when you've done all of the above and still had no success? Maybe you've just chosen 'one of those days' when it is difficult to catch any fish. The answer is return to those different places, only, this time, pick them apart as meticulously as you can. It's called 'scratching' and we'll discuss it in detail in a later chapter. But, for the moment, let's rather discuss how to 'bag-up' in the happy event of finding a group of fish.

Remember:
(When searching familiar waters)

- Go to the best places first, because you must spend the most time where you have the best chances of finding some fish.
- One of the lure angler's best weapons is mobility.
- Make the best use of the time you have.
- Keeping your lures as close as you can to the maximum number of fish is the golden rule.

(When searching new waters)

- Do some pre-planning.
- Talk to fellow anglers.
- Be flexible and change your approach and location until you find a group of fish.
- Revisit structure.

When you've done the work learning about your water and have a good idea of the best places to try, you should be getting among fish fairly regularly. And on the rare but very happy occasions when you find one or more of your good spots has a lot of fish present it's important to take advantage and 'bag-up'. We'll discuss pike in some detail first, and then look at other species.

Detection

Sometimes the reason for several pike gathering in a small area is obvious – there are large numbers of prey fish nearby. I say obvious because on a boat the sonar reveals all. But it might not be so obvious if you're fishing from the bank. Quite often there is no apparent reason for the gathering of pike – it just happens. The nicest thing though, is that if the water is clear enough then they will compete for our lures! This might seem hard to believe if you're struggling to get to grips with lure fishing, but it is true. I have a rough rule which I repeat often: 'the chance of getting a take if two pike are present is twenty times higher than from a single pike'. When there are half a dozen or more right in front of you, then you will have to be spectacularly incompetent to fail to detect one – if you follow the basic procedure of searching familiar water outlined in the previous chapter.

I chose the word 'detect' carefully. You may see a pike following your lure, but that will depend on water clarity, surface ripple and light levels. One might swirl or splash at a lure close to the surface, but you are probably more likely to feel one touch your lure. If you happen to have got the depth and speed just right, then you'll get a hit. Given average luck you'll be close enough to that correct presentation to provoke a pike to investigate, but not so close that you get a proper take. The more pike present, the more likely it is that they won't be especially choosy – it's your lucky day!

Fish the right depth

If you are going to catch a lot of pike from a spot, you will usually not be fishing very deep, but the term 'deep' is relative. Not very deep might mean 3 ft on a big river, but perhaps 12 ft on a deep clear lake. In any case, I would not expect one of these larger gatherings of pike to be close to the bottom in the deepest water. If I had to make a bet on the depth that will usually be productive, I'd say it will be just a little deeper than the depth at which you can see your lures. Eight times out of ten these gatherings of pike are feeding at a depth just out of sight of birds. I don't like to speculate about why, but I suppose that's where the prey fish are likely to be gathered. All fish seem very nervous of avian predators – which is not surprising as those that are not afraid of the flying shadow die young. Whatever the reason, fishing at a depth just beyond the distance you can see into the water is a very good place to start.

On the rivers that I fish regularly that depth generally varies between 1 ft and 5 ft. It is quite a narrow band and there are thousands of lures that will run in that band, so it should not be too difficult to find something that will be right. What is quite startling though is how picky the pike can be about exactly what speed and depth the lure should be running at to get properly hit. It could be that at 3 ft you are seeing a few pike and getting an occasional nudge, but at 3 ft 6 in, they are nailing that lure (or just as often the other way around). There is no logic or pattern to it, you have to check it and then lock on to the right presentation.

Fish the right speed

I'll relate a little tale here to illustrate the point of fishing the right speed. A few years ago I was fishing with Neil Roberts on an unseasonably summery October day. A few days earlier I'd picked up some quality pike while failing to catch any zander. I knew they were up for it so we were kitted out for pike only. We could see nearly 3 ft into the river, and caught straight away on trolled Bull Dawgs – stopping to cast only when we hooked a decent fish, ignoring the jacks. On our second stop, Neil had three pike in five casts and I didn't have one! I turned to watch – he was beginning his rather faster retrieve as soon as his lure hit the water, I'd been letting mine sink for a couple of seconds and retrieving at a moderate speed. I copied him and straight away had a fish, and another, a few casts later.

In our next spot we cast around and shared a couple of small ones, then I felt a pike bump the lure but it didn't take, when it happened again I realised I had let my retrieve lapse into a slower and deeper one. I cast back over the spot, did it properly and had a good take that resulted in a mid-double. I wouldn't forget again. We caught some more fish trolling, but it was a few stops later before we found enough to cast at. First cast I had a sixteen pounder, then, a clumsy cast produced a bump on a deeper retrieve after a slight tangle. Next cast I had another slightly bigger fish – I asked Neil to pass the net but he was busy: 'I've got a twenty following my lure' he said, so I hand-landed my seventeen-pounder. Neil's 'twenty' didn't take. I had another half a dozen fish from this spot, while all Neil had were follows and bumps. Then he suddenly realised what was going on, he had slowed his earlier retrieve speed, not deliberately, but just carelessly.

We both learned a big lesson that day. Those pike would follow or nudge lures that were too slow or deep, but if they were going fast enough and at the right depth, they nailed them. This is why I find the term 'presentation' is so useful – it's never just the lure that counts, but where it is, and how fast

Neil Roberts unhooking a pike. When your fishing buddy is busy unhooking fish while you are just casting and retrieving you had better start paying attention to what he is doing and copy it if you want to join in the fun.

it is going. This is where the analogy with stick float fishing for roach comes to mind. The fish are there and they are hungry, but you've got to give them just the right presentation before they will take the bait. It is very frustrating when you know there are lots of fish in front of you and you cannot find a presentation to turn their obvious interest into solid hits. However, as your experience grows you will begin to exploit these opportunities more efficiently, and soon add to your quota of good days.

Dealing with 'followers'

Before going on I'll give some thoughts on 'followers'. These are pike that follow the lure but do not take it. I like to keep things as simple as I can so I see it like this. Your lure and its retrieve (the presentation) may provoke a reaction in the pike. If that reaction is for the fish to follow the lure, then it is not the

Having felt a bump on a slower retrieve I remembered the lesson from the previous stop and speeded things up – result!

right reaction, so you must have got the presentation wrong. I think that eighty per cent of follows are caused by too slow a retrieve, so I tend to start with a fast presentation and work my way to slow. That's good advice in terms of catching the most fish anyway, so it should be easy to keep it in mind.

Once a pike has followed, but not taken, then it is a wary fish. If you repeat the presentation and let it follow again you merely increase that wariness, and suddenly you are wrapped up playing a silly game with a pike that is not going to take your lure, while you waste your fishing time. The first time you get a follow there is a procedure that I have found maximises the chances of getting that fish. First thing is don't tell your fishing buddy! Always be careful when you first see the follower, and fish the retrieve right in and then leave the lure, floating or sinking, a yard or so away from the rod tip – the clearer the water then the further away this should be. Now, no matter

Michel had motored quite a way to get to one of his very best swims on the River Maas where we were casting big lures for pike. On the first anchoring point Michel had two follows from two different large pike. One came in after a spinnerbait, the other chased a jerkbait – both on fairly fast retrieves. From my position I got a good look at both of these fish and I didn't think that they looked as if they were really going to hit the lures – they were just being nosey. When we moved the boat to the next anchoring point I'd decided that I was going to use a slower presentation, so I changed lures. I cast my 8 in Megabait Charlie, counted down four seconds and began a slow retrieve, and three seconds later I was in business with this tremendous beast.

what the pike does, you must resist the temptation to twitch the lure. You might think that you can 'trigger' it, I'd bet that nineteen times out of twenty you will frighten it instead. So stay still and wait. And wait. The pike will swim away calmly after a while – which can be well over half a minute but will seem like half an hour at the time! Once it has swum off you can relax. You have an interested pike in front of you – the first part of the lure fishing success story, i.e. location, is in place.

Wait a few minutes then get everything tidy; the landing net, unhooking pliers, camera or whatever. Then think about what you have learned from the demeanour of the pike that can help you to improve your presentation. Did it come late? Maybe it didn't see your lure until you lifted it at the end of the retrieve, so your next retrieve needs to be shallower. Did it come early? Well that's usually because the retrieve is too slow – perhaps it spent too much time looking at the lure before it had to decide. Whatever you do, you have to change the original presentation. Often just changing the retrieve speed/depth will do but I think changing lure usually gives you an even better probability of success. Once that pike has looked at a lure, it sometimes just gets into the habit of looking at it.

In summary, don't frighten the pike by making the lure do daft things at the end of the retrieve. Wait a while before the next cast. Don't repeat the same presentation.

Adjusting tactics: Pike

There are several things you can do to vary your presentation. Adding a little weight to the lure will do it; or if you are boat fishing, changing to a different line diameter. On the boat it is straightforward to change your rod to one with a different line or lure and I do this sometimes, but on the bank carrying an extra rod is often more bother than it is worth. Adding weight to the lure is more viable, Subtle changes such as adding a couple of heavy split rings to the hook hangers can have surprisingly marked effects on lures of near-neutral buoyancy. More drastic changes might require wrapping some soldering wire around the hook shanks, or sticking some adhesive lead to the body of the lure. If you worry about how this affects the lure's action you haven't been concentrating on what I've been writing – depth and speed control is the key to presentation and whatever you have to do to achieve that has to be done. Of course messing around with lures while you should be fishing is strictly a last resort, only to be considered when you cannot achieve the presentation you want to try any other way.

Two other simple changes in technique could be considered first – countdown time (on sinking lures) and rod tip height (for all lures). Between these two factors you can adjust to and cover a range of depths, but the range is limited, and the obvious answer to increasing that range is to change to a different lure.

Achieving optimum retrieve speed can be much trickier. It takes practice to lock yourself into the right speed, and it is easy to slip away from it. Remember what I wrote about the majority of lure anglers retrieving at the same sort of medium-slow retrieve; they do it because it is so easy. It can be surprisingly hard work to keep moving lures consistently at speed, and so easy to fall back to a slower retrieve. Having the right rod helps; a stiffer rod will make fast retrieves easier, as will using lures with less vigorous actions. Retrieving slowly, on the other hand, presents different problems, which are mostly in your head. It's hard not to think that you are not covering enough fish, and worry that you're missing out. But if a slow retrieve is right – and the fish are in front of you – you should be catching often enough to keep your concentration going. I couldn't keep the really slow stuff up all day for just a couple of fish, but it's not a problem to stay focused if I'm getting plenty of action.

Another point about fixing the depth and speed of the retrieve is to be aware that your lure's performance might change because it has taken on some water. Hollow plastic lures and

Artur Brzozowski with a spoon-caught metre-plus pike and me with another caught on a Dawg. An unusual day when we caught well but the pike were spread over an area, obviously active but not really ganged up and we had to use several different presentations through the day to keep the takes coming. Probably the sort of day when a livebait angler would have caught well because fish were moving through the area.

Dave Hilton ruefully considers his tail-less Dawg, and it's not funny – no really, it isn't funny at all! All soft plastic lures can suffer this fate so it's always smart to have a few spares with you if you are going to be catching plenty of pike.

wooden lures are prone to this, so maintaining the finish and fixing leaks on these lures is essential. Pike are also very likely to damage a lure, sometimes by penetrating the finish with their teeth on the take, but more often in the landing net, when one hook is in the mesh and the other is in the pike's mouth. This can put the lure under a lot of stress and can bend hook hangers and metal lips, which might not be very obvious, but when just a few inches' variation in depth is important they are points that need to be watched. Everyone knows that soft plastic lures (like Bull Dawgs) are easily cut to ribbons by pike teeth. They can be repaired, but that job is better done at home rather than on the river, so you need spares. With soft plastics especially, it is smart to change them before they get too battered. If a couple of inches of tail gets ripped from a Bull Dawg it won't matter, but if the body is torn in half, then the repair is a lot more difficult, so it's best to swap before the damage gets to the point where the next hit destroys it.

In September, 2008, Michel Huigevoort came over from

Michel Huigevoort teaching some English pike a few manners! He quite enjoyed getting my Dawgs chewed up.

Holland to speak at the Pike Angler's Club convention and have a few days on the river. I'd promised zander fishing only so he had brought no pike gear, yet the river was too clear for good zander fishing so we switched to enjoy some good quality sport with pike.

He looked in one of my lure boxes and said: 'All your Dawgs look like they have been in a bad accident' and then proceeded to put them through some more punishment – he was laughing because he was getting my lures chewed up instead of his!

Deciding how many spare lures to take along is difficult for the bank angler. You have limited space and you want as wide a selection as possible, so packing a dozen lures that are just spares reduces the range of lures you can carry. It's your decision, and it lies right at the heart of lure fishing. 'How many lures do I need?' is right there with 'How long do I spend in this swim?' – there's no right answer. You have to consider how many good swims you have to fish. If you only have one swim worth fishing then take the widest range possible because

James Ashworth in a hurry to hand-land what turned out to be a 13 lb pike, but the pike has other ideas.

If the lure is in sight, and it is only hooked on one point, a small fish can sometimes be unhooked without touching it. But be careful if you are holding the line with one hand to pull the fish up – you would be surprised how small a fish can break a leader when it shakes its head when it is out of the water. The answer is to hold the line loosely so if it does a big shake you can let the line run through your fingers.

you've got to get a fish from there, or you won't get one at all. If you have plenty of good spots to try, then you have to back yourself to find numbers in one or more spots – which is when you will grateful for your spares. I find on the waters I know well that I need very few different lures when I'm catching plenty, although I will need some spares. When I travel to unknown waters I take a bigger variety.

There is a danger in taking too big a variety though; it can slow down your development as a lure angler. Unless you do an awful lot of fishing you really cannot develop a high level of expertise with several dozen different lures, and you are unlikely to fish competently and confidently with lures that you only cast twice a year. Fishing a few lures very well, with accurate speed and depth control, will catch you plenty of fish and you will capitalise when you find a lot of fish – though you might struggle on really tough days because you cannot ask enough questions. It depends upon whether avoiding a blank is vitally important to you. I find it less important these days, but on local waters I know so many places that I am bound (well, almost bound) to find some fish somewhere. Having a boat makes avoiding a blank much easier because you can get to so many more swims in a day, and there is also the 'get out of jail free' card of trolling – but that's another story.

When you are in the fortunate position of having a lot of active pike in front of you the action can be fast and furious. You can expect fish on successive casts – five out of five is the best I've done – but only once. Three out of three is no great surprise. If you're fishing with someone else you have to make hay while the sun shines, so get the fish unhooked and returned quickly – the more you weigh and photograph, the fewer you catch. And be prepared to help with netting bigger fish because you might need the favour returned later.

When you are handling a lot of pike in a short time things can get a little manic, so be careful not to get sloppy when landing them. Watch out for hooks and teeth – if you get tired take a break, have a coffee or energy drink. Carelessness will definitely cause you pain!

If you take your fishing seriously, and appreciate how hard you are going to have to concentrate, you won't go out with a hangover because you are not going to be at your best with a bad headache and eyes that hurt in the sunshine! Don't drink alcohol during your fishing session either; it makes you brave when you unhook pike, and caution when unhooking pike avoids unnecessary cuts to your fingers.

While the action is fast and furious you do feel under pressure from a fishing partner, and you want that lure back in the water as soon as you can to make sure you get your share of the sport. In the first place taking care over unhooking is kind to the pike. You'll want to catch them again, so treat them well. Have all the unhooking gear ready to hand, and always be prepared to cut hooks to get them free. Making the decision to cut a hook quickly will save lots of time and no end of injuries both to you and the pike, at the cost of a few hooks. You'll need spare hooks and split rings, and they will need to be easily accessible and not in some forgotten tub in the depths of your tackle box. All these words are based on experience. I've made every mistake in the book at one time or another and suffered the consequences – I'm not preaching, just telling it like it is.

Remember to stay locked into the right speed and depth presentation or you'll be missing out. There are only so many pike available from one spot, so when it goes quiet you have a couple of options. The first is move to another swim, but you've got to be very confident that another swim will hold fish before leaving the good spot you are already on. The risk of getting there and finding it empty of pike might be worth taking if it's not too far away, if you can guarantee getting back onto the first spot later, but it's a blow to take the gamble and then find someone else is in your hot swim when you return, so it's usually best to milk the good spot while you can.

Once the initial rush of fish is over there are lots of options to help you catch some more pike. The obvious thing is try a few other presentations, but it's not the first thing you should do. I always change casting position before messing with the successful presentation. On a boat it's easy to move around and try different casting angles. From the bank it's harder, especially with foliage and weed beds in the way. Just do what you can to alter your position, even casting from the same spot but pushing the rod as far as you can reach to one side will

Michel unhooking a metre-plus Dutch pike in September 2003. You can see the firm grip he has, which will hold that pike if it starts to thrash about; it takes experience, confidence and a strong grip to do this. If you are not confident it is best to do it in the net with the fish still in the water, then if you cannot maintain the hold, the fish comes to no harm.

It depends upon the size of your hands but pike up to around 7 lb that are hooked on one treble are often easier to hand land by gripping them behind the head. It keeps your fingers safely away from hooks and teeth.

bring the lure back on a different trajectory and might show the presentation to a different fish. The other thing is to cast away from where you've had the main action – with big groups of pike there are often peripheral fish that are not in the main bunch (sometimes the biggest fish in the gang), so it's foolish to miss those casts out.

Only after checking these options, should you consider changing the presentation. I wouldn't want to change the speed and depth by much to start with, but a colour change can sometimes work, or a bigger lure of the same type that has already succeeded can be a smart idea – you won't have to make many casts, just enough to check the area. Then I'd start trying a few deeper retrieves and varying the lure type – again something different often seems to catch the biggest fish.

If you have a large enough number of pike in front of you (say, twelve or more), then during a long fishing session you will very probably catch one or more of them again. Sometimes it's easy to remember a pike if it has any unusual marking or scars, but quite often one healthy 12 lb pike looks much like another, so you might not notice. They never fight as hard the second time around though, which is a useful clue. Quite often these repeats do not hook as well on their second go either. Perhaps they are a little nervous of the lure, despite being provoked into attacking it by the competitive instinct. Changing lure colour or lure type to one that gives a similar presentation will sometimes restore the confidence of these previously caught pike. It's up to you whether you want to catch the same fish more than once in a day – I can't see anything wrong with it and it depends on your other location options.

I want to describe the nature of the competition between fish for lures that I mentioned earlier. I first saw this back in 2003 when fishing with James Ashworth. The Severn had become remarkably clear in October, and we could see the bottom 6 ft down – about 3 times the distance that we'd normally think of as clear. The pike formed gangs around prey fish shoals, and takes became quite predictable as we trolled along. The prey fish would show on the sonar, and a second or two later one, or both, of our rods would go. One morning, I thought I saw a pike following the one that James was landing, but I put it down to a trick of the light. Then, a while later, James saw one follow a fish I was playing. This was very new, what did it mean? We came to the conclusion that the following pike was hoping that the first one was going to drop its 'struggling prey' (a very visible Sherbet pattern 'Dawg) and that it would be there to catch the wounded 'fish' if it broke free. And of course we've all seen prey fish with quite substantial damage from pike. They've obviously escaped from the grip of a pike's jaws, so other pike must be used to taking advantage of this – but only in clear water. In the usual poorer clarity that we fish in it just wouldn't happen, unless another pike was extremely close by.

We decided to test the idea. As soon as one of us hooked a pike, the other made his cast to just behind where the hooked pike was being played. It was very effective, nearly always producing a hit. It makes perfect sense, but we would never have experienced it if that autumn had not been so dry and the water so clear. Sometimes, late in the winter, we get nice clarity but as there are fewer feeding pike I have not seen the same thing happen then. It is not unusual to get a hit with the fish coming off, and then get another hit that sticks a few seconds later. Maybe it's the same fish having a second bite – but it could easily be a second pike that was waiting for its chance.

Adjusting tactics: Perch

For most anglers, the other predator, besides pike, that they are likely to encounter in large numbers is the perch. Perch, like most shoaling fish, seem to require good water clarity before forming into large shoals. One difference I've found between perch and pike is that numbers of perch can turn up almost

Like many lure fishing innovations, the drop-shot has its roots in the USA where it is a major tactic for largemouth bass and other non-toothy species. It is tied from fluorocarbon line so it has no resistance to a pike's teeth – it is an effective technique primarily for perch and zander, but also for chub and trout. It is the slowest way to present a lure close to the bottom. The 'drop' distance between hook and weight can be varied so you could even tie another hook in, and of course the weight can be altered to suit depth, flow speed and desired retrieve rate.

Pike can be a nuisance, so I often have a few casts with a jig or other lure to check for any hungry pike that are present, before risking the drop-shot. That's not foolproof but it does reduce the chances of bite-offs. Using small plastics, say in the 1.5 in to 4 in range, you don't attract too many pike anyway, but if you do get bitten off, have the sense to just run a wire-rigged lure through before you retie the drop-shot and risk it again. Bite-offs happen so quickly that you rarely feel the pike. I don't think a pike is going to suffer much harm by having the single hook and short length of line in its mouth. We often remove bitten-off hooks left from other non-pike anglers, probably when they take a fish being played, or a bait being retrieved.

As to fishing with the drop-shot rig, it really fishes for itself. I tend to use it as if I'm working a worm for trout or chub – nice and easy and slow. I've seen others catching with a rather more energetic method but just remember that it is in essence the best slow presentation we have, so give it a chance to work.

anywhere. Certain general areas can be reliable for perch, but unlike pike thcy do not seem to use the same swims all the time. For us lure anglers there is a fortunate similarity between pike and perch in that if they are around they will generally make their presence known by following or hitting lures, even if the lures might not be suitable for catching them – i.e. pike-sized.

The first consideration when targeting perch is lure size – generally it should be matched to the size of the perch present. Occasionally they can be picky about lure size, sometimes preferring a larger, or smaller, lure than you might expect. Luckily for us perch lures do not take up much space, so it is easy to carry a large range in a small box. I expect most shoals of perch to contain fish of similar size, perhaps spanning two or three year classes at most. So once you have the presentation right in respect to lure size, you can catch them one after the other. Occasionally there will be larger perch present – perhaps in an adjacent (smaller) shoal that may be travelling with the smaller ones, or just coincidentally nearby. There is a chance you will see or catch one of these if they manage to beat the smaller and more eager ones to the lure. In any case you should check for their presence by casting a larger lure. The small perch may still come and look at it, and perhaps even hit it, but won't get hooked, thus giving a bigger one a chance to move in and grab it.

Perch are just as choosy about lure speed as pike, and will selectively key on to a lure at a whole range of speeds, from inching a light jig across the bottom to burning back a small spinner. I've found them to be generally less choosy about depth though. Check all depths anyway – you'll probably find one depth that is better, but it might not remain the best depth for long. When you are on song, you will get several perch chasing the lure, and it is not especially unusual to hook one on each hook of a two-treble crankbait – savour these magic moments, you'll be pleased to recall them on cold January mornings!

Old fishing books often talk about a shoal of perch

disappearing once you lose a fish. You will usually bump and prick several fish for every one you land, and soon the takes stop. They've gone! But not far – they will move a few yards, you just have to find them again. This can happen several times and you have to keep finding them – sometimes they'll just move up and down along a bank all day. Curiously, they do not seem to be put off by the lures, just the spot they were being caught from.

There are countless lures in the size range that will catch perch. If I was only taking a minimum with me then I'd have some small crankbaits in the 1.5 in to 4 in range. Long casters will help if you are on the bank – especially when you're trying to find them again when they've just moved off. Small spinners like the Mepps Comet and Mepps Aglia, in sizes 2 and 3, are good for smaller fish, but going a size bigger can sort out the bigger ones. Pre-moulded jigs from 5 g upwards, in lengths of 1.5 in to 4 in, are widely available, and often very effective. Everything small catches perch – but good-quality lures that will run true, even when you are retrieving quickly, are a must. A final point on presentation is that very erratic retrieves can be most effective – perch sometimes seem to relish the challenge of catching a difficult target.

Adjusting tactics: Chub

Chub are probably the most difficult fish to catch in numbers from one spot. Because you are usually fishing very close to them, they will spook the first time they see you – perhaps as you net your first fish. Your best hope, usually, is to build a nice bag of chub by covering a lot of riverbank, taking one or two fish from several places. You can slightly improve your chances of getting more than one fish from each spot by trying to take your fish from the extreme ends of the shoal. On small rivers they are usually seen patrolling an area parallel with the bank, drifting back down the main current then moving back upstream through the slack water or back eddy nearer the bank. Picking a spot near the turning point gives you a chance of picking off a single fish without the others seeing you land it. Chub are not fussy about lures – a light buoyant crankbait of around 2 in to 3 in will do. They will take smaller lures, but by using them, you increase your chances of getting the smallest fish, and also of nuisance perch spoiling your ambush. Using lighter lures also means lighter rods, which vastly increases the chance of the chub finding a snag as you play it, and of you being unable to stop any lunge into a sunken branch. If a match angler has this problem he leaves a little hook and a few inches of line in the chub's mouth, whereas if it happens to you, it leaves a lure with a couple of trebles attached to a wire leader, and that will mean the death of that chub if it cannot shake them free.

Mentioning wire – you need wire because very often around that shoal of chub there's a jack or two (or maybe a bigger pike) that may decide to beat the chub to the lure. Luckily, wire makes no difference to the chub. I've risked lures without wire a few times when the chub wouldn't take my lures, but they invariably didn't take them without the wire either. I thought afterwards that the chub were just uneasy. Perhaps they suspected I was there, and they hadn't bolted but had just stopped eating. If they are not frightened they are usually very easy to catch with lures, at least during summer and autumn. In cold winter water I've had very few, although I must admit I haven't tried that hard.

There are occasional opportunities to make larger catches from one spot. Weir pools, for example, can contain large numbers of chub, and you can catch them one after the other if you can cast to them from far enough away. I had some tremendous sport on Bevere Weir on the Severn back in 1995 – I had twelve in just over an hour one morning, and only two of those were under 4 lb. It was just amazing – it took longer to check the weights than to hook and land them on the pike gear I was using. The key was in getting as far away as I could from the weir, whilst still staying in casting range.

A long-casting lure was a must of course. The lure I used on that memorable morning was a Mann's 1–Minus which casts like a bomb and those chub just loved it. The astonishing thing was how hard they could hit it without getting hooked. Great slamming takes that didn't get a fish, I just kept cranking and sometimes the third hit in a retrieve would get a fish. This is another example of fish competing for lures, and of eager fish not getting hooked because they hit the lure head-on, where there are no hooks.

Adjusting tactics: Zander

If you are lucky enough to have zander in your water you'll find them in gatherings of varying numbers. Often the groups are small – from a couple of fish up to half a dozen, but quite often the groups are larger, and once in a while you might come across twenty or even more. The smaller groups tend to be of just one year class and size, but as the groups get bigger the variation of age increases, and in a group of twenty or more any size might be present.

Zander are usually on the bottom, or close to it, so a sinking lure is often best – easiest to use is a jig with plastic trailer. Deep-diving crankbaits are also useful, but any lure in the right place stands a chance, including far bigger lures than you might guess at. I've had zander as small as three pounds on a standard Bull Dawg, Some days lure size can be critical but generally 3 in to 7 in covers most situations, and most of the zander I've caught on bigger lures over the years were accidental captures when I was fishing for pike. These days I deliberately use bigger lures with longer trailers on the jigs, and successfully. Varying the jig weight gives speed options, and lure speed is, as with pike, often more important than lure type.

Persistence and determination are often key factors in getting a bag of zander. They are sometimes present in large numbers, but not hungry and can be very difficult to tempt.

When you're on fish you don't want to waste any time unhooking them. This big zander had taken the small jig well back into its mouth. The long-nosed pliers are the right tool to get a good solid grip on a hook. Being confident, firm and positive is the right way to unhook fish. This one weighed 13 lb 5 oz.

Within a minute of dropping the jig back down over the snag I was in again, and this 15 lb 9 oz beauty fought like a demon to get back into the snag.

After hand-landing countless pike doing the same with a zander seems a doddle, but it is not without its hazards. They can splash about crazily when they see the sunshine, there are still hooks to be careful of, and I've had the front spine of the dorsal fin pierce the palm of my hand a few times. Often it is far easier to net any over a couple of pounds. These photos remind me that a day spent catching zander in September sunshine makes life worth living.

We had a mission: to catch 20 zander in a session from the Avon. This meant going through all my known spots. We did make the 20 target very late in the day after catching from most of the swims, along with umpteen smallish pike, some perch and a small carp. The best spot produced one each over 9 lb before Tim Kelly won the day's gold medal with this 13 lb beauty.

Tim Kelly thinks he'll unhook this zander easily but finds the stinger is out of reach of his fingers so the pliers are quickly brought into play.

This near-double zander was the biggest fish of four taken in four casts while my boat partner was looking in his bag for the right jig.

The answer is to keep trying different presentations – by covering the whole spectrum of speeds and lure sizes you can sometimes build a fair catch, with fish caught on several different presentations through a long day, without catching two on the same lure.

Generally, once you start catching zander, you will get any others in the swim very quickly. When the action stops it's unusual to find others that respond to a change of presentation. If you have another swim to try, then I recommend moving to it rather than trying to scratch some more out, but returning to the same swim later can produce more action.

Neil Roberts with a most impressive 19 lb 5 oz zander from the Severn, caught on February 28th 2008. We had found a large congregation of zander of all sizes – this was the biggest of a boat total of 38 and the smallest would have been no more than 12 oz. Such high quality fishing is spectacular and unusual – a sound knowledge of the river and a reliable search technique meant we were able to find them and take advantage.

Remember:

➤ The chance of getting a take if two pike are present is twenty times higher than from a single pike.

➤ To get a 'follower' to take, try a faster retrieve.

➤ There are many tactics for pike, perch, chub and zander.

SCRATCHING

This chapter is where I describe how to scratch out some fish when it is tough, and it's mostly about pike. It would be nice to think that you only have to turn up and fish your lures competently in a good place to guarantee success, but we know that there are days when it can be very difficult to coax a pike or anything else into taking a lure. What can you do? What magic tricks are there to prevent a blank? It can seem to an inexperienced lure angler that most days are like this, but that is simply usually down to not knowing enough good places to fish.

Location is key

Choice of location is the first thing to consider. If you have a choice of venues then use it – simply by going to where there are some active fish is the answer. But it's often not quite that simple. You may not have any choice except the one spot, and if you've got just a few hours you'll probably only have time to visit one spot anyway, especially if you've had to travel some distance to get there. In any case, it is not that unusual to have quite widespread periods of low pike activity, with everyone complaining that they are not biting, so swapping venues just wastes fishing time.

I am not going to worry too much about why these periods of low pike activity occur. I think it's mostly down to the pike being unique in British waters in its ability to catch, in one bite, enough food to last it a fortnight. This means when there are good days when many pike are active there are going to be days when they lay low, quietly digesting their meals. We are certainly going to be fishing sometimes on days when most of

We've all seen pike carrying these leeches, and it's often on the hard days when we notice them. Active pike don't have them so I assume that the leeches get a hold when the pike are lying dormant on the riverbed.

the pike are digesting rather than catching their food, so we have to get used to the idea and do the best we can. It would be very nice to have some indication or clue as to when these very hard days will occur, but I've never been able to fathom out any pattern. You simply never know when you set out just how many pike you're going to encounter.

I do want to emphasise though that location is the key. Even with several miles of river to go at, and with the mobility of a boat, I've experienced lots of days that seemed very grim with absolutely nothing showing. However by trying lots of places I've eventually come across a group of perhaps half-a-dozen fish that were quite happy to take a routine presentation. Although still a tough day because so much of the time has been spent just washing lures, a lively 45 minutes has turned up a reasonable return for the day's effort. It is always about finding the right location – it's so much easier to catch fish when they are present!

What do you do, then, when you've been making sensible, carefully-controlled presentations for a couple of hours in your best swim – or the best swim you are going to get to on the day – and you haven't seen a sniff of a pike?

This was on opening day, 16th June 2006, and we were expecting lots of early season action but the first four swims had produced nothing. We returned to one of the swims and started working hard and after a while I caught a very small zander of maybe 8 oz. I was curious as to why it had jumped out of the water twice as I tried to reach for it ... then the penny dropped! Something must have been chasing it. Fully expecting a pike I dropped the jig back in, held it at half depth and immediately had a mighty hit and caught this 15 lb 4 oz zander, my first double on a jig. Pay attention to everything and sometimes you notice something that really matters.

It's time to start scratching – but think again about your location before you do. Are the water conditions similar to those when you have had success there on previous days? If so, then it is reasonable to suppose that there are pike present again. What if the conditions are different? On my local rivers, the clarity and flow are the key factors in determining where the fish will be. If the water is clear, they tend to go deeper, or stay in cover, such as in weed beds or beneath overhanging branches. If the river is very clear and has been for some time, then the prey fish will have moved out and shoaled up, with the pike not far behind them.

In the first case, you might need different lures and techniques to make presentations at greater depth or among weeds – the pike are still using the area but are not exactly where they usually are.

In the second case, the pike have simply gone. Many lure anglers who are used to fishing clear-water lakes and pits often feel that the big rivers I fish are very coloured when I think they are perfect. In fact lure-fishing is not made easier when there are miles of empty, clear river, unless you can find the shoaled prey fish. If the water is dirtier, all fish tend to come in to shallower water, still close to the best area, but maybe in an adjacent place that would never produce fish under normal clarity.

Perseverance

If conditions are apparently normal, then you should to stay put and start work. Do not be tempted to wander because if your best swim is not producing fish. Why do you think that going to somewhere that has never produced much in good times is a smart idea?

Firstly, think about what you've already done in an attempt to find the fish. Consider carefully the depths and speed options you have covered. Are they worth doing again? Pike move around a lot some days, and maybe it is worth trying your regular presentations again to see if any have moved into the swim. Even if on most days this is not going to work, never forget that sheer persistence is a very useful character trait for a lure angler.

Let us assume that there are going to be no fresh pike moving into your swim. So where is the first place to start to dig some fish out? I think most experienced lure anglers start to fish slower and deeper when no fish are taking and this is a natural place to start.

Slower and deeper

So, we are going to be dragging our lures along the bottom of the river, lake, or whatever. It is time to think of jigs – it was not so very long ago that jigs were considered quite novel lures in the UK. How things have changed. You can fish just about any depth and speed with a jig of a suitable weight and a plastic shad or grub. If jig-heads and plastics were the only thing you ever used you would build a high level of expertise in mastering the depth and speed control and you would catch plenty of fish.

For this special problem, though, you are going to be fishing slowly and close to the bottom. Picking the weight of the jig is the key. You are going to be retrieving slowly, and the lightest weight you can get away with will work best, because it will not snag up so readily. And it will be easier for a pike to take properly if is not weighted too tightly to the bottom.

I often prefer to use a spinnerbait for this job, because it will snag up less. It is a bit unorthodox to just drag it across the bottom so slowly that the blade doesn't spin, but it has caught me nice fish on some bad days.

I won't pretend that crawling jig-heads or spinnerbaits around is easy. It requires patience and good technique, and beginners will certainly find it quite difficult. One key is keeping the rod tip up, which helps pull the nose of the lure

All too often a hard day means a few mini-pike. Locally we notice that you never catch these when the proper pike are active. I kept my knitted gloves on to unhook this winter jack and eventually had to prise its jaws apart to release it.

The river was low and clear on 10th March 2009 and takes were hard to come by. I was fishing with Tim Kelly and we were sure there must be zander in the area. We kept working, changing presentations, and every now and then we'd get a fish but never had two hits on the same one. This example was just over 10 lb and it felt like we'd earned it – we never saw a pike all day.

over snags rather than into them. I know this goes against my advice of a low rod tip to maintain depth, but for this special technique you have to use the low speed to keep the lure tight to the bottom

Cover the water thoroughly

Covering any amount of water is going to take time with a slow presentation. But just to make it even slower, when you're scratching for fish, you need to check out the whole area that you can cover. I can't emphasise that enough.

On a bad day, I think one of the problems is that a pike will just not move very far at all to take anything, maybe a few inches if you're lucky. So you have to make sure you have passed that lure close to every pike that might be lying quietly on the bottom. Who knows, maybe actually touching a pike with the lure is the trick that will make one take it?

So be very thorough. Make accurate casts with a very small gap between each splash. There might only be one pike out there, so you had better get that lure close to it. If you have to stop a retrieve halfway back to clean the lure, then make the same cast again and cover it properly – don't move on. If you catch rubbish again, then the next cast should be aimed just short of where the lure fouled, until you find a clean run. And fish the area by your feet carefully. Lift the lure slowly, and don't forget the 'killer pause' – every time – before the next cast. If this sounds like dreary work, I wouldn't entirely disagree. It requires a lot of concentration to keep that jig or spinnerbait just moving, making accurate casts and remembering where the last cast went. This is proper fishing – it isn't about the lure but about your capacity to concentrate.

On plenty of occasions, after a prolonged period casting from the same position, I've found that I've drawn a pike into the margins by my feet. Maybe it has crept in a little bit at a time, just curious about the lure but not ready to take it, or not close enough to it to do so. It is therefore important, before you move off to a new casting spot, to lower your jig down in front of you. If the water is so deep that you cannot see the jig, then a pike might be there. Just lower it down close to the bottom and hold it there. A little movement might not hurt, but this sort of a day is probably not the one for making that jig dance about. Mind you, this is sensible advice for any sort of day, not just a bad one. Always check the water closest to you before leaving a swim where you've been casting for a while.

'Walking' a crankbait

There is another bottom fishing technique, and that is 'walking' a deep-diving crankbait. In water any deeper than 10 ft this is not going to be the answer, but for many bank fishing situations it can be done quite easily. You need the right lure – there are quite a few that will do. And you also need the right line diameter – the finer it is, the slower you can crank, and the deeper you can go. Rod choice is down to experience – a stiffer rod means you can pump the lure down to the right depth quickly, but a little suppleness makes feeling your way along a simpler task.

It is simple enough – make the cast, then drop the rod tip down. Getting it down to a couple of feet underwater (or more if you can) will help. Now crank hard until the lure hits bottom, then lift the rod tip out of the water and crank slowly, feeling the crankbait bumping the bottom, its big diving lip keeping it away from most of the rubbish.

I wouldn't describe this as an easy method, but it is probably less difficult than the jig and spinnerbait retrieves already described. When you feel the lure stop, push the rod tip back towards the lure and the buoyancy of the lure will lift it. You need to know your water – this is not a clever plan for fishing among submerged branches.

Fish with 'soft hands'

For all these bottom-fishing techniques, you need to fish with 'soft hands' because the lure is going to bump a lot of stuff on its return and if you keep striking at every tap it won't work. You have to concentrate but relax – you strike only when a fish pulls. It takes some practice, and I still make mistakes now and then, despite having spent countless hours working at these methods. You have to really tune in to what you are doing. The tricky thing to master is feeling the difference between knocks that come because you are pulling the lure into an obstruction and knocks that come when you are not moving the lure. Most of the second type are fish – but not all of them. Lures have momentum, and sinking lures sometimes fall over things and pull on the line when you are not cranking, which is most disconcerting, and crankbaits seem to have a life of their own sometimes.

With high water a constant problem in 2012 I was pleased to get out on a near-normal Severn on 22nd September with Dave Hilton. It was a strange day because we covered a lot of miles but never really found any significant groups of fish anywhere. We were sort of searching/scratching all day yet the boat total was 17 fish, comprising six zander, four pike, four perch, two salmon and a chub – in the context of a very difficult season that was a good day, yet we never really knew where the next fish was coming from.

Doing any of these presentations thoroughly is going to take time. I don't start with them lightly – I have to have exhausted all other hopes before I get this serious. I bet other experienced lure anglers use other slow presentations for fishing along the bottom, but these are the ones I stick with. They work well enough. Although going deep and slow seems an obvious option, it would be a mistake to think it was the only one – shallow and slow is also worth a shot.

Shallow and slow

In around 2005 I was guiding a client who wanted to bank-fish. When we turned up at the riverside I was delighted to see pike striking at fry. There were a lot of pike present and they were feeding – it was going to be easy! Six hours later the pike were still going crazy, we had seen hundreds of strikes at fry, often with several pike striking almost simultaneously as if the first one triggered the others. We had not had a take. I was absolutely stuck, we had been 'through the box' and every lure had been tried – admittedly I didn't see things quite as clearly then as I do now, but I was stunned, and very embarrassed. Finally my client caught a jack on a spoon, so it was not a blank, but it was a serious failure to exploit a great opportunity.

About ten days later, I was back there solo for an afternoon, and there were nearly as many pike doing exactly the same again. For an hour or so I thrashed away fruitlessly, then I stopped fishing and started thinking. I had been in exactly this situation before. Everything I tried then failed, so why should I think trying exactly the same stuff all over again is going to work? Time was quickly passing on that short February day so I had to come up with something quick. I don't know quite where the inspiration came from, but I decided to try something very different. I had a Muskie Innovations Shallow Invader that I had tail-weighted to give a very slow head-up rise when paused. This was one of the failed lures I had already tried but now it was going to be presented differently. The water was shallow, at most 6 feet deep but the clarity was quite poor, no more than 6 inches. I had previously noticed something that my customised Shallow Invader did, and thought that it was certainly different from anything else I had, so I cast out and retrieved it very slowly, so slowly that it did not wobble at all but ran dead straight, just a couple of inches below the surface. I really cannot remember the thought process that got me trying this idea beyond its being very different to everything else I'd done.

I caught seven pike very quickly, not big fish, but very acceptable in the 4 lb to 12 lb class. I'm tempted to speculate about why it worked but I won't, because such speculations are no more than guesses. Depth and speed are all that matter. In this case very slowly at just above visible depth. In the context of this chapter, about scratching when things are very tough, this is not a strictly accurate inclusion, but just once in a while some almost magical piece of inspiration can turn a 'scratching' day around. You just have to free your mind up of preconceptions and think differently sometimes. I know I keep repeating this message but it is fundamental to all lure-fishing – speed and depth of your presentation are what counts, not the lure, so if your crankbait is not wobbling or that spinnerbait blade is not turning because the lure is moving too slowly, you mustn't think it is wrong – just try it. Do whatever you can to get that combination of speed and depth right, and the fish will do the rest. They've never read a lure catalogue or seen a fishing video so they don't know that you're not supposed to retrieve it like that.

Surface lures

Surface lures can also have their uses on tough days. Quite why a pike will respond to a floating lure but refuse one an inch under the surface is something we can never know – it's all part of the speed and depth mystery. One lure type that has a knack of raising pike is a 'stick bait', or Walk-the-Dog lure. These are infuriating lures, because you only hook one pike for every two dozen that appear to swirl at them, but they do sometimes have apparently supernatural powers to make a pike show itself – and often big pike. On a day when you might only get one take, it doesn't sound very smart to use a lure with a less than twenty-to-one take to hook-up ratio, but a pike that has risen to one of these is a pike that is awake. It might go back to sleep soon afterwards (and they very rarely come a second time to the stick bait), but there's a slim chance they will respond to another lure in the few minutes after they've shown themselves.

So if you see a pike rise near the stick bait, fish the retrieve out, ending with a longer killer pause than usual to check carefully that the pike hasn't followed the stick bait in (you do not want to spook it when you lift the lure out), and then swap it for another one. Replace the stick bait with something that will run just under the surface on a slow retrieve – a floating diver of some sort, or a crankbait, or, my preference – a jerkbait with a slow rise. Fish it slow and easy. If this change of lure works, it will work within three casts, but usually on the first one. Don't expect this plan to be a banker technique every time you try it, but you should try it sometimes and think about how it might help you on easier days as well – it is very impressive magic when it comes off.

Fast and furious

On the other side of the speed spectrum is very fast. This is strictly for clear water – the fish have got to be able to see the lure. Your definition of clear water might be different to mine, but where I normally fish it means two feet visibility into the water, preferably more. If you want fish to catch a fast-moving lure they must have time to see it and react. In dirty water they just don't have enough time to detect and decide.

You could use any lure you like for a very fast retrieve, but a lipped lure (a crankbait) will dive, while a blade bait (spinnerbait or spoon) will rise.

I've found one lure that works pretty well, and that is a Bill Lewis Magnum Rat-L-Trap – only 4 in long and an ounce in weight, it sinks quickly and holds depth well on a fast retrieve. Once in a while blasting one of these through a swim will pull a pike, and quite often a pretty nice one, when all the sensible stuff has failed. Sometimes it might get a couple but it is not a presentation to try for long. You have to rely on the pike being able to see (and hear, it has a very noisy rattle) the lure and either respond or not – three casts are enough in many swims. Cast, count it down and then crank like crazy. It seems quite astonishing that it works at all, and it is not an everyday presentation. But I often give it a try before I walk away because it sometimes works when all else fails.

Another fast presentation that looks even crazier is to use a buzz-bait. This is a wire-framed lure quite like a spinnerbait, but with a prop instead of a blade. You crank dementedly and the lift from the prop keeps the lure on the surface. It looks like it is going ludicrously fast but it can work a treat, and it is especially useful for fishing over mixed weed and algae that clogs other lures.

In summary, if you cannot move to somewhere else good, then your presentations for difficult days are going to be different from your regular weapons. While it is still all about speed and depth, it is important to go to extremes.

Casting

Tough days are saved by a couple of fish – you have to fish hard, concentrating all the time and not miss anything. One department where sloppiness can soon creep in is casting – make sure your accuracy stays sharp. It is easy after four hours to feel it is all a waste of time and just go through the motions, but every time you cast, you have to decide where the cast should go and execute that cast. If you miss your target then do it again. On a tough day, say you make 500 casts – you are relying on one or two of them to produce a fish. So it's important to hit the spot, if 498 casts are right but two are only close, then if you go home blanking you might wish you had just made the extra effort to get those two casts right. The answer is that if you fail to hit a spot you cast again and again until you do. Persistence and consistency will add up to reduce your chances of failure. The casting practice will do you no harm, either.

I remember an episode about 17 years ago when I was fishing with my brother, Tony, on the Warwickshire Avon – he was not that interested in lures but keen enough. The river that day was a bit dirty, and as usual, under those conditions it was not producing anything. Then we came to a huge weeping willow on the far bank. I made my cast and got pretty close to the obvious spot and retrieved. On that tough day I was not surprised when the lure came in fishless and turned away to try the next spot. Tony, however, made his cast bang onto the bull's-eye and a few seconds later he had his pike – the only one we caught that morning. He reminded me of this in 2010 at his birthday party. It should also remind you that I have made all the mistakes that this book is aimed at helping you to avoid!

Remember:

- It's so much easier to catch fish when they are present.
- Never forget that sheer persistence is really a very useful character trait for a lure angler.
- You have to make sure you have passed that lure close to every pike that might be lying quietly on the bottom.
- Before you move off to a new casting spot, lower that jig down in front of you.
- Do whatever you can to get that combination of speed and depth right, and the fish will do the rest.

Fishing weir pools

Every angler is aware that weir pools are prime locations on rivers, and even though they vary considerably in how many fish they hold, there will usually be some to be caught. Often weir pools have complicated features to deal with like widely-varying depths and flows, and snags that could be left-over debris from when the weir was built. There are often other anglers there too, which can cramp your style.

Weir pools in general

I want to go into some detail about how to go about dealing with a big, complex weir pool, based on one particular weir pool I used to fish regularly on the Warwickshire Avon. The issues that I discuss will have relevance in many other locations though, not only weir pools. Weir pools are certainly fascinating places, but they are often very demanding if you want to get the best from them. No two are the same, in structure, flow or fish population, so you have to work them out individually. As with all the fishing I've described previously, to fish a weir successfully, lure control is paramount and will dictate lure choice.

Where are the predators in a weir pool? Anywhere and everywhere can turn up fish, and although with time, you will pick up on a couple of key places that hold fish most regularly, nowhere should be ignored. You need to put a lure into every cubic yard of water possible, so you have to know your lures and be able to read the water and its different flows. Feedback from the lures will help you to understand where the water is

A summer weir pool – you can almost smell the fish! But before you start casting have a proper look along the weir to check out for any obvious snags and pick out the different flows, then choose presentations accordingly.

running – and it is certainly not always the same under the surface as it is on top.

Your first visit to a weir can be difficult. It looks so fishy, surely you cannot fail? There should certainly be pike there along with perch and chub, and possibly zander if your river has them. But not all weir pools are equal, some are much better than others. You could start by just trying all your favourite lures (and probably losing one or two) and hope for the best. But if you've got this far with this book you should be expecting a more methodical plan. You need to try to get to know the place a little before risking your most expensive and precious lures. I always assume I'll be returning to most venues I fish, so I collect all the information that I can for use both on the first trip and future ones.

The lures that we choose for the first explorations of the weir pool might not necessarily be the ones that you will catch the most fish on, but until you have mapped it out in your head you will not be able to select lures properly anyway.

Explore from top water down

It is always smart to start at the top – it costs fewer lures!

Buoyant crankbait

Use a big wobbling buoyant crankbait that will not dive more than a couple of feet, cast it into the weir pool and feel what it does. Cast to as many places as possible, retrieve steadily and see what path the lure takes as it comes back. Try this from every casting position. You will have felt the lure wobbling as you retrieved it, sometimes it wobbled faster as the flow pulled it and at other times it hardly wobbled at all, as it rode with the flow. So after just a dozen or so casts you should have a pretty good idea of what paths the water takes around the weir pool. You might, for instance, have found shallow areas, weed, or floating debris in a slack spot, which is all very important information because they could be places to avoid or places to exploit.

Deeper diving crankbait

Next try a deeper-diving crankbait, buoyant still but with a big lip, and above all cheap. You are to some extent hunting for snags here, so the big lip and buoyancy will help you back out of trouble when you find it, while the low price will cushion the blow if you should lose it. Essentially (as with the first lure), you are trying to read the current and feel for depth changes. Again, cast everywhere, from every casting position. You will find the same shallower areas and weed again, or perhaps, if you've been paying attention, you will have remembered them and allowed the lure to float safely over them. The floating debris you will have steered around or dived under. You will have also found new slightly deeper shallows and weed.

Of course you may have caught a fish or two by now as well!

Spinnerbait

Next we turn to an inexpensive 1 oz spinnerbait – casting and counting down to do a little depth finding. Casting this into heavy flows will tell you nothing, as it will be swept away, so just use it for the slacker areas. Again as it is retrieved you will feel the current acting on the blade, buzzing harder against the flow and slower when travelling with it.

Jig

Finally the jig comes into play. These are really cheap, and it's a good job too, because you will lose one or two, and we certainly won't add stinger hooks for this exploration job.

This is just cast and countdown work, casting to those deeper areas where you have not already touched bottom with the other lures. As a sinking lure falls, it pulls the line tight, and as soon as it hits bottom you see the tension drop from the line (although in heavy winds and flows it is very difficult to spot). You may need a variety of weights to do this exploration method well. Too light a jig will get washed sideways by strong flows so do not be afraid to step up the weight to get the information you want, but remember that a heavier one will sink a little faster and that will affect your estimate of relative depths.

If you do all the above you will have a lot of information about the weir pool – far more than if you had simply made a few random casts with your 'favourite' lures. So now is time to apply that knowledge to catching fish. The flows and depths will dictate what sort of lure will be usable. The principle here is to try to get a lure into every cubic yard of water; I know this is going to be impossible for various reasons, such as casting

With clear autumn water and hungry pike it's time for some great visual action. We both saw this pike come charging in to nail James Ashworth's Shallow Dawg from a slack area near an Avon weir pool.

positions, snags, flows, etc., but it should still be the objective. Only after you have fished all the available water a few times will you know the productive spots. Lure choice is important for the usual reasons. Will it cast far enough? Will it run at the depth you want? Will it run at the speed you want? Will you be able to steer it around or over snags? Will it come through weed?

When those questions are answered you can choose which lure to use. Let's look at some of the lures I'd take to cast from the bank in a weir pool that I know very well.

Tight to the sill

There are often pike sitting tight to the sill in a foot or so of foaming water. This usually means a big cast, so the first priority of any lure chosen is range, and with one or two very visible snags protruding it needs to be able to be cast accurately as well. It also has to float, because at that range you would never be able to get control of a sinking lure fast enough to stop it sinking into the rocks. If the wind is right then there are plenty of choices, but I have one lure that will hit the range no matter what the wind is doing, and it floats – the

Cobbs Floating Glider. This lure is made of wood with a thick epoxy coat and it has survived the odd heavy impact with the concrete of the weir itself.

One thing is obvious though, the Cobbs Floating Glider is not, at range, and in heavy flow, controllable in respect of its action. It is really just a painted stick, and guess what? It doesn't matter. Those pike are not holding up scorecards to mark your ability to make a lure work well. They are waiting in that foam for any fish to be washed over the weir – anything big enough for them to see and roughly prey-sized will do. And as they have barely a couple of seconds to take it, the hits often come instantly – as soon as it hits the water, they are on.

When the lure comes away from the foam, say about three yards from the sill, I reckon it is far less likely to get a take. So as the water deepens, I simply crank it back as quickly as I can for the next cast. Doing this I work along the weir, making accurate casts maybe a foot or two apart all the way along the sill. You have to be meticulous; if a cast drops short, then do it again properly. This will take at least half an hour to do thoroughly and it is worth doing at least twice on each trip. Sometimes on my favourite weir this will produce perhaps five pike, and sometimes the only one will come on the last cast, after working all the way along – so a little dedication is required. There have been a couple of occasions when the only pike in a session has come to this presentation.

I'm sure you have heard the expression 'lures are tools, not toys' – the Cobbs Floating Glider does a specific job and I will not be using it anywhere else on the weir pool. The fact that it works tight to the sill of the weir dictates my choice, it has nothing to do with my opinion of the pike's preference – it is just the best way I know to present something in that position.

Just off the foam

Next area to check-out is just off the foam. It's a slightly shorter cast and a lot more lures are usable here – the choice is now just about depth and speed. The flow is also variable just off the foam, so one lure will probably not do for the entire length of the weir. The area is still not that deep, from around 3 ft down to 6 ft or so, and there are some larger stones on the bottom plus some weed to trap lures that run too deep. Along the weir the water does not come over evenly – some places are quite slack next to the foam whilst others are flowing quite quickly away from the sill. The very fastest flows are unfishable – the water is coming towards or across the casting position faster than you can crank, so there is no lure control. Yet the very edges of these runs are a little slower and easily fishable, but they tend to be narrow and the cast has to be spot-on, and variable crosswinds make them very difficult to hit. The main target though will be the larger slack areas between the fast runs.

The range, combined with the flows (not just where the lure lands but where the line lies across flows on the water) means that the control needed to make fancy jerkbaits dance their stuff is just not possible. You need some resistance from the lure to keep it under control.

With such shallow water (given surface visibility down to a foot or so), a pike on the bottom will easily see a lure at the surface, so depth is not a difficult issue as regards control. Any lure fished in the top half of the water will be visible to active pike, so it is a case of picking lures for speed.

This is obvious territory for the reliable 1 oz spinnerbait with a moderately fast retrieve and the rod tip held fairly high to keep the lure up, but casting range might be an issue. To give yet more speed variation you can vary the weight of the spinnerbait and the size or shape of the blade. But in such a swim as this you shouldn't need much variation in manipulating the lure, either a straight retrieve, or a sink and draw, with short pauses to let the lure drop just a foot or so between pulls, is the way to go.

Depending on how much water you are trying to cover, I would only keep these variations up until I was confident I had covered the water properly or had stopped catching fish. Some

With my back to the wind I was able to cast the bucktailed spinner into the magic spot. It dropped through the water then the blade started to spin as it felt the back flow from the undercurrent and the pike promptly hit it.

casting positions might only really need four or six casts, so why carry on? I'd assume I've done it well enough to show the lure to any pike present – if they do not want it or are not there at all what purpose is served by doing it again? So just tick it off the mental list of things to try (although there is no reason why I would not give it another go later) and look at the next presentation that you can do from this casting position.

Other sinking lures can be fished in exactly the same way, or with slight changes. One lure that I used to use a lot for this was a Lureland Spitfire – a small jerkbait-shaped plug with a small blade on the back in front of the tail hook. Fish it just like a spinner, allow it to sink to about two-thirds depth and then accelerate it into a dead straight retrieve. Often you get the take as it rises on that first acceleration, so be ready, but takes can come everywhere. Remember that there are two big trebles hanging down so it is not too smart to let it hit the bottom.

An in-line bucktail is another choice – bigger is better generally, but they can get more awkward to cast as they get bigger.

A spoon is another sinking lure that will fit into this niche, and the right one can be retrieved a little more slowly than the others already mentioned. But although spoons generally cast fairly well in terms of distance, they often plane off to one side so they have serious limitations in terms of accuracy. A Bull Dawg could be used, but because it has no 'pull' against the retrieve you tend to lose contact with it as it comes back with the flow – you cannot read the depth and speed, so it is almost bound to snag up.

Most of the time, lure choice just does not matter that much to pike. The first lure you can run properly through the slot gets

Salmo Fatso Crank is a long-casting crankbait that will stay on or very close to the surface depending on retrieve speed. It's a reassuringly hard-to-ignore lure.

the hit, or hits. Sometimes though, a little variation is needed to do the trick, especially in speed. Apart from the speed, this variation can be size or in the difference between a straight retrieve and one with pauses. Lure choice only matters in respect of it allowing you to try each of these variations. When I get several fish on one lure I don't think: 'They really wanted the "Super-duper Magnum Wiggler" today, what a great lure it is'. But rather that I could perhaps pause that lure long enough, or run it fast enough at the right depth, to trigger the hits. I will remember the position where those fish were, and perhaps the speed of the retrieve, long after I've forgotten which lure I was using.

The water just off the foam can also be covered with crankbaits, and there are rather more options here. Firstly let's consider a shallow diver, like the Rapala SSR. In these conditions it will not run deeper than 18 in even when retrieved quite quickly, because the flow is pushing it along as well.

Another in this category is the Salmo Fatso Crank. This is such a good caster that it could also be used in the foam like the Cobbs floater mentioned earlier. It runs either on, or a few inches under the surface, with a wide flapping action – a lot like a nice roach being quickly landed on chub tackle. These two options cover the 'fast and shallow' department.

To run a crankbait more slowly through this shallow water,

Fish on! A nice pike has just nailed the Salmo at maximum range and I'm bending hard into it. This was a July early evening in lovely warm sunshine and the pike were hitting almost everything I threw – Heaven must be like that.

you need a deeper diving option – just cranked very slowly. The Muskie Mania Ernie or Little Ernie will do nicely, but they will hit the bottom quickly if cranked at any speed. And while their big lips will keep them out of most trouble, if you are dragging the bottom you are often fishing underneath the pike, which is undesirable. These two lures dive so sharply that you will almost certainly not be able to prevent them from hitting bottom in this relatively shallow water – you will have to pause them frequently to let them rise a little. This is no bad thing, as four out of five takes will come as the lure rises.

If the flow is strong, be careful to keep the line tight as the lure rises. In slow or still water when you pause a crankbait and it rises what do you do with the rod? If you hold it still the lure will rise straight up, maybe rocking a little as it rises – but if you push the rod tip towards the lure, it will reverse as it rises. The bigger the lip and the greater the buoyancy, the more marked this is. So with a lure like the Ernie it will back up a long way, possibly over the head of a following pike. I think that following pike have a lot of trouble resisting this and it certainly catches plenty of fish.

Another lure to try for this job is the Storm Deep Thunder. It dives so quickly that it is probably unusable in less than 6 ft but you can 'walk' it along the bottom on the slowest retrieve, allowing it to pause and rise slowly. This is a very slow presentation, not something for searching water.

With all these lipped lures it is important to start the retrieve right. Casting at the slack water spots just off the foaming weir sill you should let them pause for a second or two (you only have a couple of seconds before the flow catches the line and drags them out of position) as pike will sometimes come up and take them just after they splash down and before they start wiggling. Now, if the strong flow acting on the line does not allow even a second's pause, the best alternative is to get the line tight as quickly as possible. Sweeping the rod hard round to get the lure to dive as sharply as you can (but not too far), and then holding it for a second before letting it rise again. Then you push the rod back to the normal position (taking up slack with the reel as you do so) and get ready for a take – because one is more likely to happen there than at any other point on the retrieve.

Although you cannot get good control of jerkbaits because of the flow, there is a chance of using one to good effect in the slack spots. A Salmo Sinking Slider has its uses here. You cast and let it sink no more than a couple of feet, then give it one short steady sweep and pause. It will dart away from the sill, then turn sideways on before the next pull as if it is turning to say, 'Chase me', to any pike that has seen it move away. It is a technique that is immensely satisfying when a pike slams the

Weir pools are, of course, homes for perch as well as pike – the same principles apply about thoroughly searching the water, but you use smaller lures.

lure after the first pull. But once you pull this type of lure into the faster flow all control is lost. So I cast, wait a second, give it a pull, pause, give it another pull and pause, then retrieve it as fast as possible for the next cast. Again it is a lot of work to fish just three yards of retrieve, but it is simply a case of keeping the lure in the best place for as long as possible – the place where its presentation is most likely to get a pike.

Sunken trees and gravel banks

If you fish the same weir pool over a few seasons you will notice that, in common with the rest of the river, the details of the flow change, as winter floods remove old features or install new ones (like sunken trees or gravel banks). On the weir pool I am describing here, two superb spots – the first a banker for quality zander and the second a real honey for double-figure pike – lasted just one season each before high water changed something that I could not see and they stopped producing.

Always be aware that these changes can take place and go carefully with expensive lures immediately after high water periods until you have checked for any nasty surprises. One spot that only lasted a few weeks was interesting. I was using in-line bucktail spinners a lot in 1999/2000, and one day, due to a miscast, I accidentally found a place where I'd landed my bucktail in water flowing quickly directly towards me. It sank for a couple of feet as I tidied the line on the reel and then the blade stared turning fiercely and the lure held position for a few seconds (obviously the flow under the surface was going backwards), and a nice pike hit it. The same spot produced good fish on several visits, but only one in a session, before it stopped working. I guess some rock had moved to create a holding spot that was big enough for just one pike, then floodwaters moved it again and the spot was no more. It is a reminder that pike can be anywhere, so it pays to periodically check even unlikely-looking spots.

Weed etc

Some of the casting positions have weed such as bulrushes, bur-reed and lilypads, in the shallow, slacker water by your feet, and of course, these sometimes hold a pike or two. Standard procedure is to cover this weed before casting at the weir. Just remember that the biggest fish in the river might be hiding in those weeds – do you really want to find that out when it misses the lure you are lifting from the water for a recast? Or when it bolts as you clumsily land a jack? Always cover the water by your feet first. Something else can happen here though. After a period of casting and retrieving from one spot, a pike may have followed your lure, or perhaps seen it from the side and moved in to take a closer look. If it has, it will eventually settle down in or near the weeds and at some point such a pike will have a slash at your lure, so be ready.

Slack water and eddies

There are slacker areas and slow back eddies in the vicinity of the weir pool and these have to be searched as well. One of these is on the far side, a good cast away. It is deep over there, from a line of reeds the water slopes quickly down to 11 ft. But to add some complication there is a sharp change in depth about halfway back where any deep-running lure will get into trouble, as the bed rises quite quickly to around 6 ft. Plus there is quite a strong flow over this shallower run and the depth then stays constant right back to within a yard of the bank.

A change in depth is a very important holding feature – such a deep slack adjacent to fast-flowing shallower water is generally a good place to look for pike anywhere on a river. Pike are either in the deep slack, or, more often, holding somewhere on the drop-off between the fast and slack water, and they can be extremely choosy about just how they want the lure. Depth control in such a difficult swim is vitally important, so lure choice comes down to a lure or lures that offer easy control in that respect.

Deep water

A sinking lure is obviously a smart choice to cover the deep water on our illustrated weir pool, but getting it over the rise is problematic. And because the riverbed material on the rise is clay (into which your lure will stick at the slightest touch) and there are also some mussel beds and the odd branch which occasionally takes up temporary residence, you need to take care. There is a way though – just remember the count back system I described in the 'Lure Control' chapter (where you count the turns of the reel handle).

A spinnerbait is first choice because it has the best chance of coming through the hazard, so cast it out to the far reed edge, tighten immediately and allow it to fall to about 8 ft. Then retrieve slowly to maintain the depth until it hits the rise, counting the turns on the reel handle as you go. It's dead easy. And suddenly you have a very powerful piece of information – you can choose to lift the spinnerbait over the rise at any distance from the rise, and on different days this will make a difference. Sometimes getting it tight to the rise and sometimes lifting it up and over, well away, will do the trick. And as you will know exactly where your lure is in relation to this feature, when you get a take you will know exactly how to repeat the presentation to pick up more fish, or how to change the presentation and try a different line. This control is vital for consistent success.

The other obvious lure choice here is a deep-diving crankbait – the Ernie or Little Ernie again coming into play. You won't get either lure to hit the bottom of the deeper water, but there is no need to – close is close enough, I'd say that they would get down to around 8 ft at that range, but it depends on how you retrieve them. To get the most depth from a deep-diving crankbait you have to really accelerate it. The easiest way to do this is to have the rod pointing at the lure, then on a tight line, and keeping the rod tip as low as possible, sweep it quickly and powerfully around to the side and really pull that lure down. Then, if you want to get another couple of feet of depth, push the rod tip back quickly, whilst taking up the slack, and give it another sweep. This power dive, apart from getting the lure deep, is also a big trigger to pike. It's amazing how often the take comes a second after the sweep stops – as you are tightening back up – so be ready and have your rod in position to strike hard.

A couple of things can make this less effective. Too short a rod reduces the dive, and too long a rod can get caught in bank foliage. So sometimes a little bank pruning can help make the long rod more usable – this big pull and pause is such an important part of crankbait presentation that it is worth doing. Bank side pruning could be as simple as slashing at nettles and brambles with a landing-net pole, or snipping individual stems with your hook cutters (you could take secateurs, I suppose, but your hook cutters will do).

Because this power dive is such a good trigger we should give a little thought to how we apply it. Instead of casting tight to the reeds and diving it immediately every time, it can be pulled gently a few feet and then powered down, and so on, so you can cover the whole of the area with the power dive. Again, though, the position of the lure in relation to the rise in the riverbed has to be considered. Takes often come at the point when lure reaches the bottom of the dive and starts to rise on the pause, so it's important to vary where you start the pull so that any pike lying anywhere in the target area gets to see that key trigger, up close. It seems especially important sometimes to collide with that rise in the riverbed (and the depth at which you hit it can also be vital) – above all, you should be thorough and meticulous and not stop until you are sure you have hit all the spots.

Lock cuttings

The lock cutting must not be ignored because, occasionally, several fish hold up in there and there are usually one or two. Often there will be a 'No Fishing' sign – these are generally meant to stop the average bank angler setting up his array of gear and getting in the way of boats locking through. For a lure angler it only takes a few minutes to see if there are fish there, and you can easily move if a boat turns up – chances are that if it is busy lock there will be no pike there anyway.

The depth of the cutting will be the minimum required to allow boats to pass through – this can be as little as 3 ft. The turbulence from the boats' wash will generally prevent heavy weed growth, so it should be a simple matter to cover the cutting with any shallow-running lure. If the water is deeper, a spinnerbait would be useful to cover it at all depths, but if it is coloured as well, then a slower option is more likely to succeed.

It will have taken well over two hours for me to have covered all the options the weir pool offers, even if I haven't had to spend time unhooking fish. What now? I do it all again. It is

This photo dates from around 1991 when I was lucky enough to have a productive weed bed on my local stretch of the Severn. Note the fixed spool reel, and no braid back then so lure losses were high. This weed is unbranched bur-reed, Sparganium emersum. *In slower-flowing water it lies flat on the surface creating lots of shady hiding places – it can provide some interesting fishing and also teach you a lot about pike.*

just like fishing your good swims along a stretch of riverbank in rotation. Things can change very markedly in a lot less time than it takes to fish the weir pool properly. Think of each spot as a swim – pike will move in and out, or switch on and off, according to all the usual mysterious whims that control their behaviour.

Fishing weed beds and margins

Fishing shallow weeded margins for pike during summer and autumn provides the most visually spectacular fishing available in Europe – for anglers on the bank or afloat. You can often see the pike take your lure, or miss, or just come cruising in to take a look. It's a very different sport to watching a float bobbing around, or waiting for an alarm to sound. I've always enjoyed this type of lure fishing so I've spent a lot of time over the years trying to get the most from it.

It is easier in some respects than most lure fishing to get right – simply because you can usually see your lure. But getting the most from it requires some thought and effort. I've seen far too many lure anglers shy away from fishing weed because they cannot work their lures properly, and keep getting snagged up. But that's a big mistake, because weeds can hold large numbers of pike, and it's a case of choosing the presentations that will work through the weed – not complaining because your favourite technique and lure is unusable.

Big lures, tackle with backbone

Before you start fishing around or over weed beds you need to consider what tackle and lures to use. Firstly, you need lures that are quite big, simply because, if you're like me, you'll want to give yourself the best chance of attracting big pike. And once you've attracted one you'll need a strong rod and braid that will pull it quickly from dense weed.

For such thick line I'd use a multiplier reel. Relatively thick braid tends to prevent a lot of casting problems, because it does not bed into the spool so easily, and is rather nicer to handle than thinner stuff – especially when pulling on snags and weed.

The choice of rod is not too vital – around 6 ft 6 in to 7 ft 6 in is nice, but it must have enough backbone to stop a pike quickly before it can bury itself too deeply in the weeds. Of course the strong braid plays another important part here – pike are not hard fighters (compared to carp, say) and in open water you can land even a fairly good one quickly enough on relatively modest tackle, but in a weed bed things are very different. Even the softest weed can have tough roots, and there may be submerged branches in there as well. These hazards could help your pike to escape, often simply by knocking the lure free, or by catching hooks in them and tearing itself free, and sometimes, more seriously, by cutting the line through on some rough edge. So you need stopping power in your rod, and you have to have the clutch of your reel set properly. Far too many lure anglers set their reel clutches too lightly, as if they are frightened to bend their rods. The right way to set the clutch is to clip your leader to something solid, like a gatepost, then bend the rod into it. At maximum compression (with the rod bent to 90°) the clutch should not be letting any line out; that way you are using the full shock absorbency of the rod to take the sting out of the fish's lunges. Only if the fish is strong enough to pull the rod down hard and straighten it slightly, will the clutch allow some line out. This will tame even large pike very quickly and prevent them from diving away into weed. Of course, the leader wire, swivel and clip will have to match the strength of the line – or you'll soon find out why!

Lures

Now to the lures – you don't need too many for weed beds, because you are fishing such a small depth band. Also, you don't need any with fancy actions like glide baits, because you'll never be able to work them through the weed (although a very shallow runner could work over the top of submerged weed). After a few trips you will soon be able to make sensible judgements about what sort of weed beds can be worked with what lures. This comes down to a few factors, but the density of the weed is the most obvious. If it is contiguous, i.e., with no gaps, then you are not going to have many choices, but the most productive areas usually have a few gaps.

The second feature that limits your choice is how much of the weed reaches the surface. If it tops out a foot or more down, then it makes life easier. I've enjoyed good sport sometimes fishing weed beds when there have been a few inches of extra water on the river, and I can easily run lures across the top of the weeds. But usually the weeds are touching the surface.

The final factor that makes a difference to your presentation options is the species of weed. There's no need to get all botanical here but there are a few obviously different species that have different characteristics, and these characteristics change what you can do with your lures.

Let's start with a couple of lure choices – the spinnerbaits and the shallow-diving crankbait.

Spinnerbaits

A spinnerbait, with its single in-turned hook, should be an obvious candidate for fishing weed. I nearly always fish from a boat, but weed beds can usually be fished quite effectively from the bank – if access is available. The big difference between fishing from boat versus bank is that from the bank you don't have the choice of casting angles. Also you'll probably have to cast further, and you'll probably lose a lure once in a while, even with the strong braid.

A golden rule is to catch the closest fish first. Just because you can cast forty yards it is not compulsory to do so. Make a few short casts to check that there are no fish close to you that will be scared off as you land a fish that you hooked further out. I know it's the umpteenth time I've mentioned it – it's important!

As soon as the spinnerbait hits the water start turning the reel handle. There's no time to allow the lure to sink into the weeds. If you feel the need to look at the reel to check the line after every cast, you are going to get snagged up a lot, and miss the many fish that take as (or just after), the lure splashes down. Beginners will not be able to do this as consistently well as someone who has done it countless thousands of times because it only comes with experience and practice – and the awareness that it is absolutely crucial.

Retrieving the spinnerbait is simple enough, but also simple to get wrong. I usually use a fairly brisk retrieve with spinnerbaits because I find it stops the pike from messing about with follows and all the other shenanigans – they don't have time to do anything but grab. It is important also to keep the rod tip high, to stop the lure from running too deep. This may look rather less stylish and serious than the usual rod tip

This spinnerbait has a ¾ oz head so it is easy to keep it high over weed but it still has good-sized hooks, in this case 6/o Sakuma Mantas. The light head means a small blade, here a #7 Indiana – too big a blade will cause too much torque and twist the whole lure onto its side on the retrieve which looks horrible but probably makes little difference to a pike. For fishing in denser weed I'd take the stinger off if it was getting snagged too much. The big pike over the page was caught on a stingerless one – frightens me to think of it now. I'd also certainly not use the stinger for bumping through the decaying winter weedbeds as described in the Scratching chapter.

down position required to work some lures, but it is essential for proper control and to help the spinnerbait ride over stray weed stalks. Holding the rod at 35°/45° up from horizontal is about right. It will still give you plenty of 'lift angle' to strike and to turn a hooked pike. A longer rod makes this much easier, modern baitcasting rods of around 7 ft length are ideal.

I'll usually just run the spinnerbait nice and straight, but it pays to let the lure pause (just for a second or two) and fall slightly over any clear patches. Pauses are important in any retrieve and I bet that at least 50% of takes come when a lure is paused.

One last thing – in the chapter on 'scratching' I mentioned dragging spinnerbaits along the bottom. This presentation will

My best Severn pike to date, weighing a handsome 24 lb 4 oz. I was casting a spinnerbait and retrieving fast over weed. I did the killer pause as the lure came into view and suddenly the long green shape was in and gone, and solidly hooked. Never, ever, forget the killer pause.

also work in weed beds but the weeds do not make it any easier. Keep that rod tip high and go very slowly. Picking the right rod for the job helps. You need lots of feedback through the action of the rod, and you need some hook-setting power. Remember that the blade will not be spinning – if it is then you're going too fast. You should be aiming to keep the lead head in touch with the bottom, once that blade spins you have lift and it is not the same presentation. I've used this successfully at all times of the year, but I've found it to work best in late autumn and winter, through weed that is dying back. There's not a pike alive that will tolerate a spinnerbait tickling its nose when it is lying under weeds quietly having a rest.

Floating crankbaits

Once I'm satisfied that I'm not going to catch any (more) fish with the spinnerbait, I'll cover the weed bed again with a floating crankbait. The retrieve has to be slower though, because a fast retrieve simply dives the lure down into the weed. A slow speed may also work with the pike that didn't respond to the fast spinnerbait presentation. There are countless lures you could use for this job, but you actually need very few and it is important to understand why you need them.

I'm going to compare a couple of readily available well-known lures that fit into this category, but before I do, I'd like to make clear that I don't sell lures or work for any company that does. All the lures I mention here or elsewhere in this book are lures that I have bought myself and used.

One of the best known shallow diving crankbaits is the Rapala Super Shad Rap (or SSR for short). When retrieved, it will run maybe down to 2 ft or so on a very fast retrieve. Most importantly it is very buoyant. On a slower retrieve it will be just under the surface, and at an even slower speed it will wobble gently across the surface.

Another shallow-diving crankbait is the Bucher Shallow Raider, which is not as buoyant as the SSR and runs just a little deeper. What this means when fishing a weed bed is that you have to retrieve it more slowly than the SSR to run at the same depth.

So here you have the essence of why you choose between different floating crankbaits – the depth and the speed of the retrieve. You can make an adjustment to the running depth by how high you keep the rod tip on the retrieve, or you change lures if you need a bigger adjustment. I hope you realise from this that I feel that these two crankbaits offer very similar presentations, but when one is taking fish that the other is not, you should not be thinking that one lure is 'better' than the other, but that one of them is running at the right depth and the right speed.

Just for a moment, moving away from the weed bed, you should have a set of crankbaits that, with some sensible use of rod tip height, will allow you to cover every depth and speed option down to around 8 ft for open water. As you get deeper you have to go slower because you cannot quickly retrieve crankbaits with big lips. Grasping this simple point helps you to appreciate why you need to have to have different lure types, and how important it is to understand their capabilities and limitations. You simply cannot cover every depth and speed with one type.

Running depth

It is quite noticeable when fishing shallow water and weed beds, how a small difference in running depth can make a huge difference to results. I think the difference between three inches and six inches below the surface in shallow swims sometimes matters far more than the difference between eight feet and ten feet at greater depths. Time and time again this has proved to be the case, and I stopped worrying about why a long time ago, but I make sure that I check it out. Speed is always important with any lure retrieve, and careful control of speed marks the difference between good lure anglers and the rest.

You are always limited in your options by the nature of the weed bed – the species of weed, its density and how close to the surface it grows will prevent the use of many lures. But few weed beds are completely homogeneous – they tend to be patchy, with a lot of variation in growth, so you can fish around the densest areas with some variety of presentation. Tight lure control involves lifting the rod to guide the spinnerbait over any higher pieces of weed, or slowing the crankbait retrieve to allow it to float over any hazard.

Bank fishing

If you're fishing from the bank you are going to be restricted in your choice of casting positions. Even if there are fishing platforms, the ones over weed beds are often the first to fall into disrepair and the unused paths down to them become overgrown. A pair of waders can be very useful – they are great for protecting your legs as you force a way through the nettles, and you can stand in the water if there is no platform. The disadvantage of wading is that your low position, when standing in the water, is not good for seeing fish or submerged weed. But that's the price you have to pay and you should, anyway, have made a proper reconnaissance from the top of the bank, to give you an idea of the shape of the weed bed and the position of any obvious subsurface snags.

Wading

Wading can be hazardous. So use your landing net pole as a wading stick, and constantly check for holes and sticky patches. It's easy to fall over when you become seriously stuck in mud, so it's best to keep out of it. You might consider wearing a life jacket or buoyancy aid when you explore a new stretch – it may sound a little extreme, but you're far more likely to get into trouble wading than you are to fall out of a boat. And your unhooking tools should be either secured to your clothing with a lanyard, or attached to some floating foam. They always sink when you drop them, and even in just a couple of feet of water, will be difficult to recover.

A key advantage of wading is that you can often cover quite a good stretch of shallow water without having to clamber back up the bank. Pike can be lying very close to the bank in these swims so be sure to cover the water immediately in front of you before you wade into it. In general, short casts will help you to control your lure better and to guide it around or over weed and other hazards.

Handling weed hook-ups

From time to time you are going to get hooked up on weed – it's unavoidable. This happens most often when the lure lands on top of the weed, so accurate casting will avoid a lot of trouble.

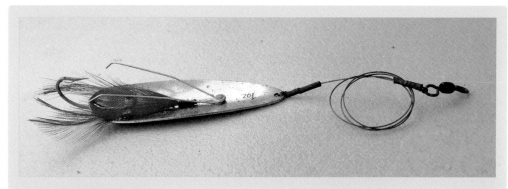

This weedless spoon will come cleanly through some pretty rough weed. Note that I have it permanently wired to its own leader with the wire twists sleeved in shrink-tube. This prevents weed from collecting around the lure clip. These spoons are not great hookers but they will get takes from places where no other lure can go. This is especially useful around Canadian pondweed on gravel pits.

When jerkbait meets weed this is what happens. In this case on a gravel pit the Potamegaton pondweed has brought the retrieve to a premature close. You can't hurry multi-hook lures through weed, and if you do get hooked up the impulse to rip the lure free usually produces this sort of result.

However, getting hooked on the weed might be annoying, but it's not a disaster. Your instinctive reaction is to try to rip the lure free with a sharp wrench with the rod, and I've read loads of times that this is the best thing to do. But this generally results in you having to pull the lure in to remove the weed that you have ripped off, and is a serious waste of time.

There is a much better way. If you maintain a very light pressure on the lure (not enough to bend the rod), then alternate that slight pressure with a loose line a few times, it will often gradually come free, without collecting any camouflage, and you can continue with the retrieve.

One huge plus with this trick is that you'll be pleasantly surprised by how often a pike will hit the lure while it's still stuck on the weed and not moving! I've had some good fish this way, and on some days the only fish from an area has come when I've been caught up.

If you think back to the basics of lure presentation, and that having your lure near a fish is the most important thing, then it shouldn't come as too much of a surprise. You might wonder then if I ever deliberately hook weed to check if the static lure is going to get a pike. What do you think?

I've only mentioned two lures so far, a spinnerbait and the buoyant shallow-diving crankbait, there are of course other presentational options.

Deep divers

Sticking with the crankbait theme, you can try a deep diver. I know it's not obvious but a buoyant deep diver, fished very slowly, can be used through some terrible weed, especially lily pads. You keep the lure on the surface and retrieve it so slowly that it barely wobbles at all. The wobble is really not important, and trying to keep it wobbling will just stop the presentation from working, because the lure is travelling too fast. The big lip pushes a lot of weed out of the way, and as soon a you feel it bump weed (you should not be retrieving so fast that you hook weed on the first touch) you just go back to the release technique – a little soft tension then a little slack. It's amazing what sort of a jungle the lure will come through.

If you believe that action is vital and you like your lures to be wobbling a bit, then you'll hate this method because the lure has no action to speak of. But if you like catching pike, and aren't too worried about what your lure looks like, then this will keep you very happy. The lure I usually use for this is a Musky Mania Little Ernie. I think a rattle helps although it won't be making much noise at the dead-slow speed, but it will be enough to attract a nearby pike's attention.

Remember, again, the need for strong tackle and powerful rods for this. A big pike hooked in the middle of a dense lily pad bed will want some pulling, and there will be a lot of chopped-off pads floating away when you look back up after releasing your fish.

This is slow and peaceful lure fishing that requires intense concentration. And when the peace is suddenly shattered and a short, tough and spectacular battle begins, you have to be ready – it's not the time to discover that your reel's clutch is not properly set.

Buzzbaits

At the opposite end of the speed spectrum is the buzzbait, which is very similar to a spinnerbait except it has a prop instead of a blade. These are not easy things to get on with – they require very fast retrieves that are hard work, but you can fish them across the top of virtually any weed. Even if there is filamentous algae present, which tends to catch on every other lure, a buzzbait will usually do very nicely. A lot of anglers who think they know pike do not retrieve a buzzbait fast enough, so just pretend you've never read a word about lure fishing, and crank yours as fast as you can – it will not catch a pike every day but it will catch some (not just jacks) that you could not catch with anything else.

Weed beds are great teachers, some of them regularly contain pike, and even if your lures cannot be made to work 'properly' in them, you can catch loads of pike. After catching enough pike in these weed beds with your lures not wobbling properly, the penny will drop, and you will at last be free of worrying about the action of your lure and concentrate on exactly where it is and how fast it is going. When you reach this stage it really is 'welcome to lure fishing'. You are now free

Rob Tomlinson fooled this very lean 17 lb 1 oz Severn pike by slowly and carefully working a jig downstream through a sparse weed bed.

of 'wiggle mania' and can start to catch loads of pike (and all the other species).

Jigs

Another lure that can be worked through weed quite easily is the jig. In this case a stinger is out of the question so you are relying on the single hook. I like a long-shanked jig hook for this job and not too big a trailer – say 5 in maximum. A heavy jig will get snagged too often so a maximum weight of around ¾ oz is about right, but usually rather less will be required.

The retrieve is similar to the spinnerbait retrieve, with rod tip held high. You are trying to get the jig into the faces of pike that are not prepared to come up out of their hiding places to take lures fished over their heads. Takes are often very gentle. The idea is to drop the jig right in front of the pike so it simply has to open its mouth to take it – for a second you think you are hooked on the weed, but then the weed pulls back!

One final tip

There is one final thing that might make working a weed bed easier. On a river the weed will all be laid one way by the flow so it will always be easier to work any lure with the flow after casting upstream. It makes no difference to the fish, but means you spend less time caught up. The only problem with this is that the flow will tend to define your lure speed, and it might be too fast.

If you have some pike in your weed bed you should be able to catch them. It will help you immensely if you don't fret about the action of your lure and just get it near some pike. I've gone into some detail here and you should have noticed that we have covered the whole range of 'search, bag and scratch' modes in just one swim. If you have a load of good weed beds to try, then don't start scratching until you have tried several, but if you only have one, then stick it out and try everything. A weed bed is the one type of swim where you are most likely to magically turn a tough day into a good one, by finding that one of your scratching presentations suddenly turns up lots of fish.

Remember:

➤ Lure control is paramount and will dictate lure choice.

➤ It is always smart to start at the top – it costs fewer lures.

➤ When exploring water with a crankbait you are trying to read the current and feel for depth changes.

- When fishing just off the foam in weir pools, the main target will be the larger slack areas between the fast runs.

- Four out of five takes will come as a floating lure rises on the pause.

- Weeds can hold large numbers of pike.

- To fish weed beds successfully you need big lures and tackle with backbone.

- A small difference in running depth can make a huge difference to results.

I've written about searching for fish, catching them when you find them, and catching some when you can't find them, but perhaps the most crucial skill of all is being aware of just where you are in all three modes. On most days you spend a certain amount of time in all, or at least two of them. In complex swims like a weir pool, or a weed bed, it sometimes feels like you are going through all three at once. If you can remain clear in your head about just which phase you are in, you can then use your time most effectively.

Time is not a frequent lure fishing discussion topic but it is vitally important. You have only so many hours to fish in a day and you have to spend some of that time not fishing while you move between swims. How long do you spend in each swim? How many swims should you try? These two simple questions have rather less than simple answers.

Work quickly

Whichever mode you are in, it's important not to waste time. If you are searching, you should work quickly and move as soon as you have a negative answer to your question, which should be: 'Are there loads of fish here that I can catch easily?' As soon as you know that this is not going to be the case, you move on.

But when you find numbers of fish, you change to 'bagging up' mode. To work a swim effectively you should fairly quickly be able to work out the key presentation – then keep catching, until there are no more fish. When things slow down you might try a few close variations around what has worked, and maybe a couple of extremes (of speed and depth) as well, to pick up any peripheral pike. But be careful not to spend too much time on this because if you've found one good place with a number of fish then there are probably other good places that will give you another bagging opportunity.

If you try several good places and fail to find any concentrations of fish – I am assuming that you are fishing decent places with a proven track record – then you have to resign yourself to slipping into the 'scratching' mode.

Be effective

Knowing just where you are in the different modes means you can stay focused, and use your time effectively. I know, and hope you realise, that it is sometimes difficult to tell quite what mode you are in. You have to try to keep a careful eye on things.

If you have been 'bagging' but have not had a fish for half an hour, then that mode is over. You can go searching for another bagging opportunity, or you can dig in, and scratch around an area where you know there were fish. This can be a subtle call requiring a fine judgement. Like, where is the next place, similar to this one in terms of depth, flow, weed-growth etc., that you could expect a few other fish to be present? If you have another one half-an-hour away or less, then get moving. But if there is nothing similar nearby then stay put and start scratching – or maybe rest the swim for half an hour, and let your returned fish settle.

It is not something that I could ever prove, but, given my experience with competing pike, you might have caught so many of the pike from a particular swim that it reduces the possibility of one competing against another moving to a lure. But if you give your returned fish time to recover, then their return to 'active duty' might trigger any remaining pike to respond to your lures.

When not to move

It should be uppermost in your mind that you do not move away from a gathering of pike, even if you've probably caught most of them, unless you are very confident of moving on to another concentration. When you have located some, you must milk the opportunity for all its worth, because there are plenty of days when it does not happen. If you catch a couple of them twice (which happens often enough if you stick around), they are still fish, and if they happen to be big ones, I'd be surprised if you were bitterly disappointed.

This basic rule – of staying near fish that you've caught if you've nowhere better to go, applies differently to the other predator species. Perch will invariably move away from you, so you have to keep moving to stay in touch. Chub, once spooked, will stay that way for quite a while – about 'twenty minutes to the pound' according to Richard Walker's old analysis. And that sounds about right, so you might as well go and look for some more and return later. With zander I'd generally say that once the action stops it is usually better to move on and try to find another pack.

Learn to keep quiet about your success

Most fishing success comes down to having enough good quality swims to fish. I'd swap a hundred lures for a good swim, because frankly there are that not many. Many good swims remain good for years – if you can avoid over-pressurising them, and can be discrete enough not to reveal your 'go-to' spots to other anglers, who might not be as careful as you are not to over-fish them.

Other good swims can work for a season or two and then switch off, but may come good again a year or two down the line. I fish many miles of my local rivers, yet in over 30 miles I know of only four really great pike swims. One is well-known to many anglers, although I doubt that many really understand its significance. I've never seen another pike angler in the others, and I've no intention of letting any of them see me catching in them, either! Incidentally, none of them can be fished from the bank.

In addition, I can aim at maybe another thirty pike swims that can provide good sport under certain conditions. I am careful not to spoil any of them by over-fishing. It is a fine judgement to assess how much pressure a good spot can take. I try to vary how hard and often I fish each spot, so I can rely on getting a fish if I need one – most frequently to brighten up a day for a boat partner who has struggled.

When to call time

When considering the 'call' you should soon realise that time management is the key. I have a principled objection to looking at a watch when I'm fishing, because it reminds me of work, but I have reluctantly accepted that a watch is an essential tool, because you have to be aware of time passing.

As you switch through the modes of 'search', 'bag' and 'scratch', time does matter. When you're bagging you can forget it – just keep on catching. But time spent searching and scratching has to be controlled. I mentioned earlier about how the dead slow retrieve on my special Shallow Invader turned a scratching day into a nice success. This does not happen very often, but this sort of turn-around from despair to exultation is going to come along from time to time. So imagine the scene – it's midday already and you've blanked, then you try some slightly oddball idea and suddenly you catch four fish in ten casts, then after half an hour, no more. Now what? Your oddball idea worked so quickly that it was obviously pretty desirable to the pike, and obviously you caught everything you were going to catch there in very short order. So move – try that presentation everywhere you expect to find a pike.

If you are in search mode, how long do you carry on searching? Because if you spend all day searching for a group of co-operative fish, and fail to find any, then you might reflect that in one or two of the best swims, you should have tried a little scratching. This is the test of your judgement and your knowledge of the water. I feel that with pike fishing (provided I am not in a clear water situation with just one big group of fish

We'd gone out onto the Avon to catch zander, and we were struggling but Dave Hilton picked up a low double pike because he'd cheated and brought some pike lures. There was no point persisting in failing to catch zander when the pike were up for it, but I only had zander kit. I searched through my small crankbaits and remembered how we used to get occasional decent quality pike on the Cotton Cordell CD7 when trolling for zander on the Severn, so I tried that. Twenty minutes later my good memory was rewarded with this fat pike that went a few ounces over 20 lb.

somewhere, perhaps miles away) that if I've tried a few places I have an idea about what is going on. What I learn from two or three good swims will be enough to tell me what I should do next – like whether to burn a load of fuel and time hitting my very best spots, or dig in and focus on working the nearby swims very hard. I don't know if I get it right all the time, but I catch enough fish most days, so I feel my calls are pretty good.

Complications of targeting other species

Zander are different – it is much harder to tell from fishing a few swims what is going on with them. There may be a few fish in each swim, or most of them may be empty, with a few big groups of fish congregated in a couple of swims. Even if I find them quickly, I still don't know how the day is going to turn out. Perch are more like pike, in that getting a few means you should get some more – but they do choose all sorts of places

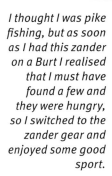

I thought I was pike fishing, but as soon as I had this zander on a Burt I realised that I must have found a few and they were hungry, so I switched to the zander gear and enjoyed some good sport.

to 'set up camp' for the day, so a good fast presentation for finding them is important.

Mentioning the other species adds another complication to the call. If you are only set up to catch pike with big lures, then if you don't catch a pike, you go home blanking. But if you have a second rod set up for smaller lures, you might be able to turn a bad pike day into, say, a good perch day.

When I first started lure fishing, for at least five seasons I tended to use mixed tactics, trying to catch whatever I could. I'd use the same spinning rod to cast all my lures. The bigger ones were a bit of a handful, and the little ones didn't cast very far – but it seemed the best I could do. I switched between all the local species, but often found myself spending a lot of time trying to catch chub. Mainly because they are, in the first place, easy to catch with lures, but perhaps more importantly, I could see them, and at least had the certainty of knowing where they were. I didn't grasp that at the time, and if I had understood how to search for pike in those days, I'm sure I would have spent far less time tormenting chub.

When I got properly interested in pike, after my first trips on a shared boat, I realised I had to use larger lures and heavier

Two days later the river had risen and coloured a bit, but I was delighted to find that the zander were still there.

rods. My boat partner was no lure fisherman and only wanted to fish for pike with baits, so the boat was always (we hoped) near pike. Fishing more determinedly for pike meant that I caught more and learned more. The light rod was not forgotten but certainly not used as much.

Things turned around again when I got my own boat, and could carry several rods and lots of lures – multi-technique, multi-species days became the norm. As I explored the river, I learned how to use the boat properly and where I could expect to find fish consistently. It was surprising how often I caught four species on one day – pike, perch, chub and zander. Oddest of all though, were the days when I caught three species, but could not find a single pike. Now that I have a fair degree of competency at fishing for pike and zander, I sometimes take all the gear out, or sometimes just kit out for the one species.

Specialising

In retrospect, I can see that the single rod, multi-species set-up did me no favours – it was too easy to just change species, and not face up to the challenge of finding the pike. And the reason I didn't do well with pike was simply that I had failed to understand about locations, and how you have to find numbers in one place to catch them. I had read too much about the 'lone hunter' pike and Mr Crabtree 'X marks the spot' swims – stuff that was, and still is, totally wrong.

Adding a choice of species to the mix of 'search', 'bag' and 'scratch', does not necessarily make life any easier either. It will add complications in tackle requirements, as well as in having to try the different swims used by each species. If you have the time to fish a lot and develop good skills with more than one species, it will be easier to have good days by switching between species, but a beginner can easily end up doing nothing very well and failing twice over. If your water offers good fishing for one species there is good sense in specialising. Then, once you have become competent with the one species, it is not difficult to learn about another. The core skills, and good habits of accurate lure control, will already be in place – all you have do then is apply them to different lures in different locations.

The overall approach I've outlined, of just getting your lure close to as many fish as you can and then doing whatever it takes to make them bite, works everywhere – in freshwater or the sea, and for all species. Only the details of lures and tackle change, everything then depends on where the fish are and where you are standing.

Remember:

- Time is not a frequent lure fishing discussion topic but it is vitally important.
- Keep quiet – be discrete enough not to reveal your 'go-to' waters to other anglers.

I wrote earlier in this book that I think catching fish consistently with lures is a tough discipline. It takes some time to understand lures and tackle, then a lot longer to learn about catching fish. There are things that you can do to speed up the learning process – you're reading this for a start – and so you know that you can read articles and books that may help you. You should read everything you can, even about species that you do not fish for in countries you will never visit. Try to filter out the advertisements and get to the essence of what is going on – the essence will always be about the location of the fish and the depth, speed and size of the lure.

Read with an open mind

You can read lots of articles where the author hardly mentions location, depth, speed and size, probably because he assumes you already know that stuff – or maybe he's just selling lures! There might be useful extra information about tackle – the rods, reels, lines, wire and stuff that will make the presentation easier – you have to sift through it all to find important details. Really useful stuff can be buried in amongst loads of fluff, so having the patience to find it and the sense to identify it will help you try to work out what the key factors are allowing the author to catch enough fish to write about.

Learn through experience

You won't catch any fish while you're reading, so you have to get out there and cast some lures. Just choosing where to start is a tough enough. Here are a few simple things to bear in mind:

first, go to where there are some fish. Not just somewhere that looks 'fishy' but a place where you've seen the fish you want to catch, either by just watching the water or by seeing other anglers catch them. If there are other anglers around it won't hurt, because if you see them catching it encourages you. It is easy to say after a blank session that the fish were just not feeding, but there are relatively very few days when there are none to be caught. If someone else is catching and you are not, then watch and learn, ask questions, or at least change what you are doing.

Finding lots of fish is everything, but you may not have highly productive waters near your home, so you have to just do the best you can. You are very unlikely to find big concentrations of fish on a canal or small river, but you will notice, over time, how some areas produce more often. So sticking to a single water for a lot of your short session fishing makes sense, because you will be able to take advantage of your knowledge to stay near the most fish.

Travelling here and there at random means you're spending most of your time exploring new venues, which means you're spending a lot of time washing your lures in empty water.

Learn from other anglers

Fishing with other lure anglers will speed up your learning process. You might bump into one or two other lure anglers on the bank (far more likely to happen now than ten years ago) but your best chance of finding some like-minded company is to join the Lure Anglers' Society. You can then attend one of their friendly fish-ins or competitions, where you will see anglers of varied abilities and experience trying to catch fish using a wide variety of presentations. You can fish alongside them and see how you compare, or you might learn more by just walking around and talking to everyone. See who is catching the fish and how they are doing it, keep asking questions, keep thinking about the key factors of location, speed, depth and lure size. If your tackle and lures cannot match their successful presentations, then you might decide to invest in new gear – at least here you can see it being used, and someone might even let you try theirs.

Make as many friends as you can, talk to everyone, and listen to everyone. Talking is just like reading articles, every now and then in amongst the stories and the banter, something someone says will stand out. They may not even realise its significance, but you store it and think about it, see how it fits in to your fishing – it could be something really important or just a time-saving tip, it all adds up.

I've tried in this book to get across my experience to save you time in working some stuff out for yourself. I've been lure fishing a long time and there cannot be many mistakes that I haven't made. Everyone goes through the same process, and everyone knows something useful. No matter how successful you become and however much experience you have, there is always someone who knows something you don't that you can use to improve your results.

Another benefit of fishing among lots of other anglers is to keep your own results in perspective. If you've caught a few and think you've had a good day and done as well as you could, you might be surprised to find that quite a few anglers have done a lot better than you. Or maybe you've found it hard going but your few fish are a far better catch than most have managed. Keep asking questions – find out how the more successful anglers caught their fish. But don't dismiss those who have failed, because they might have been doing something you were considering yourself, and if it has failed for them you can have some idea of how it would have worked for you.

As I've emphasised, the foremost essential factor for success is the presence of fish. Try to keep in touch with what is going on generally in fishing circles and which waters are turning up lots of fish. A network of fishing friends will help, so will reading the weekly angling press, magazines and watching out online for what is getting forum members excited. You may

When you have to teach a complete beginner how to catch a fish it helps you focus on the absolute essentials. Here my daughter Alana proudly shows off her first jig-caught zander.

have to travel some distance to visit the good waters, and that might mean a more expensive day out than you can normally afford. This raises a couple of questions. To make the most of such an investment, would you go at the weekend so you can see the most anglers fishing, or in the week when you have more space to yourself? It's a difficult call – I suppose it depends upon how confident you are. If you think you will be able to catch lots, take the weekday. If you think you'd benefit by seeing fish caught by other anglers and where and how they are catching them, then choose the Sunday every time.

Pick the brains of a professional guide

Fishing with a guide can be a useful short-cut to success. If he's any good, he'll not only put you near some fish but also help you to get the presentations just right, and you get to use the right tackle for those presentations. You are paying him, so make sure you get as much out of the day as possible. Do what he says carefully, and if you can't, then get him to show you how, and keep asking questions about those essentials of location, speed, depth, lure size – at least then if the fishing is not so hot you've still gained some value from your day.

Fish with more experienced anglers

The surest way to learn fast is to fish with better lure anglers, i.e., anyone who catches more than you. You've got to be prepared to watch these guys unhook some nice fish while you don't, but that's the price of education. If there are a lot of fish around, you will learn fast – just copy whatever the catcher is doing. But be careful – just copying the lure is not enough. You have to match the presentation – the correct depth and speed. If your tackle (rod length and line diameter in particular) is different you may not be able to match the presentation exactly with the same lure, but keep working at it until you can catch at the same rate.

There is no magic to this – there is always a measurable reason why one angler is catching and the other isn't. Quite small differences in presentation can make a big difference to catches – the successful angler, having tried a few things, has locked-on to the right presentation; it's up to you to try to match that. As you work to match it you might even find something that is slightly different that actually catches faster than your mentor. Then, if he's on the ball, he'll quickly start copying you.

I first started getting serious about lure fishing on trips with Seb Shelton. We learned a lot together and I think for both of us the penny dropped at about the same time, realising that the lures are not the most important part of the game.

Learn with a fishing buddy

I like having company when I fish, and I want both of us to be catching. Having a fishing buddy of similar ability frees me up to fish properly for myself, knowing that there is another presentation being done properly nearby which can speed up the search process. On the other hand taking absolute beginners out is often interesting, because it makes me focus on the real essentials and keeping things as logical and understandable as I can. Plus it's always rewarding coaching people who are keen to learn.

Friendly competition can be a good driving force towards making progress and catching lots of fish, but of course you're going to share the fish. You've got be able to enjoy it when your pal is weighing his trophy. After all it will be your turn soon enough (or at least it should be). If not, don't simply put a run of poor results down to luck – there may be other factors at play.

The downside

I've fished with a lot of different people over the years, and some of them I will never fish with again.

There's the chap who always has to have first cast into every swim. If only a couple of fish are going to come out in a day, then the chances are that those first casts are going to count.

Then there is the one who is a bit slow with the landing net (the worst crime of all) and it costs you your best fish.

And there is other behaviour that can make you regret your

choice of company – like when a week after a successful trip you see pictures on your favourite internet forum of your 'buddy' and his other mates holding nice fish obviously caught in the swims that you showed him. Or a detailed description of how to fish effectively with a lure that no-one else had so far sussed out.

This happens most often when someone has an outstanding day (for them) and they want to show off to build up their own credibility on the forum. Lots of people who never make any postings will read forums, always on the look-out for new good places to fish, so you have to protect your good locations and be careful of the background in photographs that you plan to show anyone. Really good quality fishing is hard to find and does not last indefinitely. It is part of Nature that predator and prey populations go through cycles, so when you have found some really great fishing, milk it for all you're worth. The fastest way to put an end to it is to share it.

The moral of the story is to pick your fishing partners with care. It only takes one trip (lasting usually less than an hour) to find out if they are 'first casters' – you have to sort it out there and then, so suggest you take it in turns and see what the reaction is. Good landing-net etiquette means that when your buddy yells 'Net!' you stop whatever you are doing and get that net to where he wants it. You need each other to play your parts when required, because you haven't gone out just to net and photograph your buddy's fish. Also, make it clear before a trip with a new buddy that if secret swims or techniques are later publicised then it will be the last trip you share. The word to remember is 'team'.

The positives

You need trust to build up a good team ethos. You've got to give a little to gain a lot, and my experience tells me that two of you co-operating will catch at least three times as many fish as either of you on your own. What does co-operating mean?

Fishing in Holland with Michel Huigevoort is always a great adventure but watching Michel hand-land this huge pike in June 2005 will always stay fresh in my memory. I'll never see a bigger pike.

James Ashworth was my most regular boat partner from 2002 until 2008. We learned how to fish the Severn and Avon together. I'm sure he won't forget fishing the Avon on the 3rd of March 2008 when he landed this 18 lb 6 oz zander, and then a couple of hours later he added a 22 lb 6 oz pike to complete a stunning brace.

Tim Kelly is always pushing things on technically and is very fast to identify what is working on the day, tweaking the presentation to further improve catches. This fine zander was caught on Grafham water.

The first time Neil Roberts met me I was furiously cranking a buzzbait across the surface of the Avon near Pershore. He obviously thought he was watching a lunatic until a nice pike nailed that lure. Ten minutes after I mischievously took this photo, he was landing the 19 lb 5 oz zander shown in the Bagging Up chapter.

Since 2009 Dave Hilton has been my most regular boat partner. He had to endure some tough lessons and watch me land a lot of fish while he came to terms with what is required to catch fish regularly with lures on a demanding river. I'd say that this excellent midwinter zander is a fair reward for his efforts.

It shows most when you are searching for fish. Lure choices should be complementary, and you have to agree how fast you're going to move – a couple of casts per swim, maybe? A few more? On a fast search you need to use lures with similar retrieve speeds. But casting from a drifting boat try one fast and one slow – one using a spinnerbait and the other a jerkbait can make more sense, so think about it and decide together.

Also if fishing from a boat, the speed of the boat dictates what lures can be used – so you both have to use presentations appropriate to the boat's speed. To save arguments, you can take it in turns (maybe on the hour each hour) to decide where the boat goes and how fast. As soon as something starts working, you'll both agree what a great plan it was!

When you get among fish, you both have to get a fair crack of the whip. If one casting position is producing all the fish, then take it in turns, changing after every fish. I know plenty of lure anglers who wouldn't want to do this, but it builds up a bond of trust that pays off over the long run. No doubt you will still be competing, but now it will be a fair competition.

When fishing from the bank, you do get some space to yourself, which is nice – but a boat is a very small space that will test any friendship. I've found that thinking in terms of the 'team' makes for more pleasant days and more fish to share.

If you can find good fishing partners that you can trust, the learning curve will be a little easier to climb, and you will have a lot of great fun and some shared memories to talk about in your old age.

Remember:

- Whatever species you lure fish for, wherever in the world, the essence will always be about the location of the fish and the depth, speed and size of the lure.

- Two fishing buddies co-operating will catch at least three times as many fish as either of you on your own.

So that's it, then ... The key is realising that a lure is just a bait, and that different lures allow you to make different presentations – different combinations of speed and depth. Instead of thinking of one lure as better as or worse than another, just compare the presentation. Perhaps it might help to think of a roach livebait. Sure, it's a live roach, no matter what you do with it, but changing the depth on the float's stop-knot changes the presentation – and that's really the equivalent of changing your lure.

All you have to do is be in control of what you're doing, pay attention, change what you're doing when it is not working, and repeat what you're doing when it works. That is the simple objective you are trying to achieve but it can be a complicated road to reach that destination, and you cannot learn it all in a few trips.

You have no excuses now – you know what you have to do, so just put this book down and go lure fishing!

Tight lines

Another fine September dawn and another hunt begins. Let's go and find some fish!

AFTERWORD

I've read plenty of books about lure fishing. Some have been rather more helpful than others but so many get so wrapped about the lures themselves that the important stuff about fishing with them is almost ignored.

The book that really opened my eyes to why predatory fish choose and use the places they do, and how they relate to the underwater topography, was *Spoonplugging: Your Guide to Lunker Catches* (1973) by E. L. 'Buck' Perry. *Spoonplugging* is not what you'd call an easy read but it contains the most important information about fish location that you will ever see in print. It took me a while to understand how to apply its lessons to my home waters, but once I'd got it I was flying, and with that understanding came an appreciation of how to find fish on unfamiliar waters. The book is well out of date in respect of tackle and the use of sonar, and plain wrong about how the size of lure doesn't matter, but it is still essential reading.

The second book I recommend is Dick Pearson's *Muskies on the Shield* (2001). I believe Dick coined the phrase 'time on the water' and it shines through his writing. His deep understanding of how the muskellunge relates to structure in different types of water under different conditions and according to season is an example of the depth of knowledge to which we should all aspire in trying to understand any predator's behaviour. I found his pragmatic use of lures and presentations was also very refreshing after reading so many books filled with baloney about lures. Never mind that you will probably never fish for a muskie, this is another 'must read'.

The third book is not as important, but *What Fish See* (1999) by Colin Kageyama did help to stop me fretting too much about lure colours – because lures can certainly look very different underwater when compared to the beautiful object you see in your hands.

My final note is about units of measurement. In this book I decided to stick with Imperial units. I'm more familiar with them, as are friends of my generation, and I was certainly not going to clutter up the text with metric equivalents. When I started fishing with lures the USA was the inspiration and the place to purchase ones that were not available in the UK, and they also use inches to measure their lures. Today it is less clear-cut because of a much stronger European influence. Fishing with lures in Europe has become very popular – in fact far more popular than in the UK. The conversion though of millimetres or centimetres to inches is pretty simple.

I would like to point out though that, quite often, European weights, especially with jig-heads, do not exactly match Imperial weights. The most striking example that I recently came across was some 2 oz jig-heads I bought from a North American source that were (much to my delight) heavier than the 50 g European equivalents – about ¼ oz heavier in fact, which made quite a difference. It may never matter to you but it is worth bearing in mind.

The one exception to Imperial units in the book is my mentioning of 'metre' pike – I do so purely for my readers on the continent because in mainland Europe a pike of one metre in length is a fish to aspire to, whereas in the UK most anglers prefer to have a target weight, rather than length.

A Reading List of Books on Lure Fishing.

A list of books wholly or mainly on the subject of fishing with lures. In addition to these there are many more books on more general fishing for pike and other predatory fish, some of which cover lure fishing in some detail. Also there are books specifically about lures, and many American books on lure fishing.

Most of those below can be found on the website of my publisher, Coch-y-Bonddu Books – www.anglebooks.com

Alfred, H J. *A Complete Guide to Spinning and Trolling, by "Otter."* Alfred & Son, London (1859).

Becker, A C, Jr. *Lure Fishing.* Barnes, New York (1970).

Barder, R C R. *Spinning for Pike.* Arco Publications, London (1970).

Bettell, Charlie. *The Art of Lure Fishing.* Crowood Press, Marlborough (1994).

Bucher, Joe. *Joe Bucher's Crankbait Secrets.* Krause Publications, Wisconsin (1999).

Cederberg, Goran & Hansen, Jens Ploug. *The Complete Book of Spinning and Baitcasting.* Swan Hill Press, Shrewsbury (1988).

Craig, C W Thurlow. *Spinner's Delight.* Hutchinson, London (1951).

Craig, C W Thurlow. *Baitmaker's Delight.* Hutchinson, London (1953).

Holgate, James. *Lure Fishing for Pike: Volume 1. Tactics and Techniques for Spoons, Spinners and Plugs.* Published by the author, Lancaster (1987).

Holgate, James. *Lure Fishing for Pike: Volume 2. More Tactics and Techniques for Spoons, Spinners and Plugs.* Published by the author, Lancaster (1988).

Holgate, James. *Catching Pike on Lures.* Published by the author, Lancaster (1991).

Kageyama, Colin. *What Fish See: Understanding Optics and Color Shifts for Designing Lures and Flies.* Frank Amato, Portand, Oregon (1999).

Ladle, Mike & Masters, Jerome. *Tactical Pike Fishing.* Crowood Press, Marlborough (2009).

Ladle, Mike & Casey, Harry. *Lure Fishing: A New Approach to Spinning.* A & C Black, London (1988).

Lumb, David. *Pike Fishing with Lures: A Modern Approach.* Published by the author, Preston (1996).

Nobbes, Robert. *The Compleat Troller.* T James, London (1682).

Pearson, Dick. *Muskies on the Shield.* Waite Park, Minnesota (2001).

Perry, E L "Buck." *Spoonplugging: Your Guide to Lunker Catches.* Hickory, North Carolina (1973).

Prichard, Michael. *Pocket Guide to Spinning in Fresh and Saltwater.* Collins, London (1984).

Rapala. *The Rapala Fishing Guide: Secrets from the Pros.* Minneapolis (1976).

Rapala. *The Rapala Book: Predator Experts Tell Their Plug Fishing Secrets.* Vaasky, Finland (1998).

Rickards, Barrie. *Spinners, Spoons and Wobbled Baits.* A & C Black, London (1977).

Rickards, Barrie. *Modern Lure Fishing.* Crowood Press, Marlborough (2008).

Rickards, Barrie & Whitehead, Ken. *Plugs and Plug Fishing.* A & C Black, London (1976).

Rickards, Barrie & Whitehead, Ken. *Spinning and Plug Fishing: An Illustrated Textbook.* Boydell Press, Woodbridge (1987).

Salter, T F. *The Troller's Guide.* Carpenter, London (1820).

Scott, Jock. *Spinning Up To Date: Trout, Salmon and Pike.* Seeley Service, London (1937).

Spencer, Sidney. *Pike on the Plug.* Witherby, London (1936).

Webster, Gary. *Spin-fishing for Sea Trout.* Crowood Press, Marlborough (2008).

Webster, Gary. *Spinning for Salmon.* Robert Hale, London (2010).